W9-BNV-075

ALWAYS BE READY

EQUIPPING YOUNG PEOPLE TO DEAL WITH UNBELIEF

KYLE BUTT

Apologetics Press, Inc.
230 Landmark Drive
Montgomery, Alabama 36117

© Copyright 2014
ISBN: 978-1-600631-01-6
Printed in China

Cover by Rob Baker
Layout and Design by Jim Estabrook

All rights reserved. No part of this book may be reproduced in any form without permission from the publisher, except in the case of brief quotations embodied in articles or critical reviews.

All Scripture quotations are from The New King James Version of the Bible, unless otherwise specified. Copyright © 1982, Thomas Nelson, Inc.

Library of Congress Cataloging-in-Publication

Kyle Butt (1976 -)
Always Be Ready
Includes bibliographic references
ISBN-13: 978-1-600631-01-6

1. Existence, attributes of God. 2. Science & religion.
3. Apologetics & polemics I. Title

212—dc22 2014947382

DEDICATION

This book is dedicated
to people whom God loves
but who refuse to love Him—
with the fervent hope
that they will change.

Table of Contents

Introduction
. . . . 1

Chapter 1
Treating Atheists With Respect 3

Chapter 2
Have You Read the Bible? 7

Chapter 3
One At a Time 11

Chapter 4
Who Wants that Kind of Faith? 19

Chapter 5
Are Atheists More Moral Than God? 27

Chapter 6
Is God Immoral for
Killing Innocent Children? [Part 1]. 33

Chapter 7
Is God Immoral for
Killing Innocent Children? [Part 2]. 43

Chapter 8
The Bible and Slavery 51

Chapter 9
The Bible and Women 57

Chapter 10
Evil, Pain, and Suffering 67

Chapter 11
Can a Loving God
Send People to an Eternal Hell? 75

Chapter 12
"Creation is Untestable" 83

Chapter 13
"All Religion Is Bad Because Some Is" 87

Chapter 14
"Christians Can't Even
Agree With Each Other" 91

Chapter 15
"Creationists Don't Publish Their Research in
Scientific Journals" 95

Chapter 16
"Everything in the Universe
is Made of Matter or Energy" 101

Chapter 17
All the Smart People 105

Chapter 18
Never Enough Evidence 109

Chapter 19
Conclusion 113

ACKNOWLEDGEMENTS

Special thanks to our Creator,
for providing an abundance of evidence
that leads all honest hearts to Him.

Once Upon a Time...

Introduction

If you had asked my youth group in high school 20 years ago if we knew a person who claimed to be an atheist, you would have gotten a lot of blank stares. Out of 40 of us, some of us **might** have known how to define the word atheism. But I am confident that less than two of us would have known a person who was an atheist. In fact, I've been working in Christian apologetics for many years, and I would guess that the first time I met someone who claimed to be an atheist was about 15 years ago. Atheism was virtually unknown where (and when) I grew up. Sure, there were kids who did drugs, had sex, stole, and committed a host of other sinful behaviors. But there were virtually no kids who claimed not to believe in God.

That was 20 years ago. Fast-forward 20 years and the situation in the United States is very different. For the past several years I have taught Bible class for the 15-18 year olds at summer camp. A few years ago I started asking the question: "How many of you know someone who is an atheist?" The first year I asked, out of the 42 kids I had in class, 32 of them said they knew an atheist. The second year I asked, 30 out of 40 knew an atheist. Some even mentioned that they had friends who were atheists. The third year, about 40 out of 52 knew an unbeliever. After one class, a young man explained to me that he was not sure he believed in God and thought he was an atheist.

As you can see, things have changed dramatically since I was a teen. Due to the fact that your generation has access to the Internet, you are flooded with ideas, both good and bad. Twenty years ago we didn't hear about atheism, because there were so few atheists and they had no real way to spread their message. The number of atheists in the United States has increased, but not greatly. They are still a very small minority in this country. But their numbers are on the rise, because they have used media outlets like the Internet to spread their teaching. They don't plan to stop, either. One leading atheist named Dan Barker described himself as an atheist "evangelist." He said: "I can now literally say that I have taken atheism to the ends of the Earth." He stated: "If we can divert just one young mind from going into ministry or from wasting time and money on religion, we have made the world a better place."[1]

Of course, nothing could be further from the truth. I repeat his statement only to show that atheistic evangelism shows no signs of slacking up any time soon. That is why you need the ideas presented in this book. The apostle Peter explained to Christians that we must "always be ready to give a defense to everyone who asks you a reason for the hope that is in you, with meekness and fear" (1 Peter 3:15). If the stats are right, your generation is being bombarded with atheism and skepticism more than any generation in the last 220 years of United States' history. You must be ready to defend yourselves against the false, destructive teachings of unbelief. Arm yourselves with the truth, be strong and courageous, and fight the good fight of faith.

Chapter Notes

1. This is taken from Dan Barker's book *godless*, pp. 320 and 324.

Treating Atheists With Respect

The idea of atheism is as false as any idea ever was. God has provided more than enough evidence to prove He exists. Those who reject this evidence will have to answer to God. But we as Christians must bear in mind that people who have chosen to be atheists are still people. They were made in the image and likeness of God. Yes, it is true that they are enemies of the cross of Christ, and many of them are attempting to teach error that is very harmful. We need to remember, however, that Jesus instructed us to love our enemies (Matthew 5:44). When we have discussions with atheists, we should listen attentively and respectfully and let them know we value them as people. We should firmly and boldly disagree with their ideas, but do so in a kind way that shows them we care about their souls. Instead of saying hateful things and being mean, we would do well to follow the advice of Paul, who said: "Let your speech always be with grace, seasoned with salt, that you may know how you ought to answer each one" (Colossians 4:6).

Some "Christians" think that atheism is such a bad sin that they can be hateful and mean when dealing with atheists. This is not true. There is no sin so bad that Christians have the right to be mean-spirited and hateful. When those who call themselves Christians exhibit such attitudes, it only helps atheism spread. For example, a few years ago, an atheistic group sued the government over a

cross that they did not want displayed. A spokesman for their group appeared on *Fox News* and stated his atheistic position. Numerous people wrote comments on Facebook about the atheists. Those comments were mean, hateful, and unloving. Here are some examples (with the spelling errors included):

> "To all atheist die an go to hell haha if I could I would shoot you all in the head with a 12 gauge."
>
> "Shoot em. At least we know where they're going, waste of oxygen."
>
> "I can offend them with a Louisville slugger to the back of their heads."

In addition to these statements several others used cuss words that we won't repeat here.[1]

What do you think the atheistic community did with these statements? You can guess they had a heyday with them. They plastered them all over their Web sites and bemoaned the unchristian attitude of American Christianity. I think we can all agree that such hateful sentiments do not express the love that Jesus instructed His followers to have for their enemies. While it is true that all those who disobey Christ will be lost forever, Christians should never express the idea that they are glad atheists or any other group will be lost. Sure, Christians should always be ready to give a defense of Christianity. **But it is often the case that those who oppose Christianity are just as interested (or more) in how you handle yourself when you defend the truth as they are in what you are saying.**

One excellent example of how kindness can influence an atheist comes from a man named Penn Jillette. He is a famous atheist who stars on a television show on HBO called Penn and Teller. In one YouTube post, Penn tells a story about a man he met after a show. This man approached him in a kind way and gave him a small Bible. The Bible had a brief note in the front and several phone numbers that Penn could use to get in contact with the man.

Penn explained that he thought the man knew he was an atheist and was trying to proselytize (or convert) him away from atheism. About the man he said:

> He was really kind and nice and sane and looked me straight in the eyes and gave me this Bible.... He was polite and honest and sane and cared enough about me to proselytize. Now I know there is no God and one polite person living his life right doesn't change that, but I'll tell ya, he was a very, very, very good man. And with that kind of goodness, it's okay to have that deep of a disagreement.[2]

Penn's reaction to this man's kindness says a lot about how a person's approach can open the door to a meaningful discussion.

It is true that most people, including atheists, don't care how much you know until they know how much you care. We have been called to love our enemies and bless them, even (and especially) when that is not how they treat us. Don't misunderstand me. I certainly think we are supposed to refute error and boldly stand up for the truth. But even when we are standing for the truth and refuting error, we can show the world that we love them, we care for them, and we don't want them to be lost.

CHAPTER NOTES

1. These are taken from an article written by Austin Cline. It is titled, "Fox News Viewers Want to Kill Atheists." You can find it at the following Web address: http://atheism.about.com/b/2011/08/06/fox-news-viewers-want-to-kill-atheists.htm.
2. This video is about five minutes long. It is on YouTube at the following address: http://www.youtube.com/watch?v=ZhG-tkQ_Q2w.

Chapter 2

Have You Read the Bible?

Since 2008, the Atheist Agenda, a student organization on the campus of the University of Texas at San Antonio, has hosted an event called "Smut for Smut." The group offers to give a free pornographic magazine to everyone who will trade in a Bible or other religious book like the Quran.[1] In 2012, a video clip posted of the event showed one of the members of the Atheist Agenda confronting what appeared to be a fellow student. This fellow student was holding up a sign in protest of the event and in support of the Bible. The atheist attempted to explain why his group equates the Bible with pornography. The fellow student disagreed. The atheist then asked the student, "Have you read the Bible in its entirety?" The student shook his head almost imperceptibly, and in a very low voice admitted he had not read the Bible. After that, he tried to walk away as the atheist followed him, explaining to him all the alleged "horrible things" found "in the Bible" that the young man had never read.

The fact that the young man had not read the Bible utterly demolished any credibility he may have had. Of course, the atheist was misrepresenting what the Bible says. In no legitimate way does the Bible compare to a pornographic magazine. But the young student could do nothing to defend the Bible, because he had not read it. Suppose that question were asked of you? Could you respond that you have read the Bible? Or would you be shamed into silence

and forced to walk away as you listened to an enemy of God revile His precious Word. How in the world can Christians always be ready to give a defense to everyone who asks them a reason for the hope that is in them,[2] if those Christians have not read the Bible?

Life By the Book

In Romans 2, Paul explained to the Jews that their sinful lives were causing the Gentiles to speak evil of the God of Israel. He scolded them in harsh terms when he wrote: "For 'the name of God is blasphemed among the Gentiles because of you.'"[3] In a similar way, the modern skeptical community delights in pinpointing "Christians" living sinful lives, or being so apathetic to the teachings of Christ that they do not care enough to read the Bible. Let it never be said of you that your stand for the truth was rendered useless to the cause of Christ because you could not honestly say that you have read the Bible.

Several years ago, George Gallup Jr. and D. Michael Lindsay produced a book titled *Surveying the Religious Landscape*. The book consisted of several religious polls taken from the last 70 years of American culture. The authors concluded: "Americans outshine most other industrialized nations in religious fervor."[4] On the heels of that statement, one survey showed that 84% of Americans believed that Jesus Christ is God or the Son of God, while only 46% of those in Great Britain believed the same.[5] Furthermore, in 1998, 80% of Americans polled said that they believed the Bible was the actual or inspired Word of God. Such statistics show that Americans, by and large, at least mentally accept the importance of religion, God, and Jesus Christ.

When questions about godly living were asked, however, the results of Americans' religious fervor did not match their **professed** beliefs. For instance, when young adults ages 18-29 were asked if they believe premarital sex to be wrong, only 1 in 4 said they considered it to be wrong.[6] That means, 75 out of every 100 young adults in the United States do not think that premarital sex is wrong! When this question was posed to the American population: "Do you think it is wrong for unmarried couples to bear children out of wedlock, or not?" 50% of those polled said they did not think it was wrong.[7]

Many young people in America **claim** to believe in God and the Bible, but they fail to put those beliefs into practice in their lives. Gallup and Lindsay said:

> Gallup research would indicate that the greatest chink in the bulwark of American religion is the lack of spiritual practices and disciplines **actively exercised by religious adherents.** Consider, for instance, the following statistic: 93% of Americans have a copy of the Bible or other Scriptures in their household, yet only 42% of the nation can name even five of the Ten Commandments. **Spirituality in America may be three thousand miles wide, but it remains only three inches deep.**[8]

We cannot hope to have an impact on any atheists if our lives do not reflect the teachings we profess to believe. Think about how it must sound to an atheist to hear a Christian say that he believes the Bible is the inspired Word of God, but the Christian does not consider that message important enough to read it on a regular basis. Think how hollow it must sound to an atheist when a Christian claims that objective morality comes from God, but that very Christian has sex with her boyfriend or gets drunk on the weekends.

In the book of Ezra we read that the prophet "had prepared his heart to seek the Law of the Lord, and to do it, and to teach statutes and ordinances in Israel."[9] In the same way, if we are going to impact the skeptical world for Christ, we must seek the Law of God, practice it in our lives, and then we can successfully teach others the truth.

Chapter Notes

1. An article about this by Billy Hallowell, titled "Atheist Students Encourage Christians to Exchange Their Bibles for...Pornography," was published in a magazine called *The Blaze*. You can find it on the Web with the video embedded in the article at: http://www.theblaze.com/stories/2012/04/03/atheist-students-encourage-christians-to-exchange-their-bibles-for-pornography/.
2. 1 Peter 3:15
3. Romans 2:24
4. *Surveying the Religious Landscape*, 1999, p. 119.
5. *Surveying the Religious Landscape*, 1999, p. 123.
6. *Surveying the Religious Landscape*, 1999, p. 98.
7. *Surveying the Religious Landscape*, 1999, p. 127.
8. *Surveying the Religious Landscape*, 1999, p. 48.
9. Ezra 7:10

One At a Time

"The Bible is so full of mistakes, I don't even know where to start," Jared casually stated over a cup of coffee with his friend Julianna.

"I certainly don't think so. I'm a Christian and I believe the Bible is God's Word," Julianna responded, trying to keep an irritated edge out of her voice. "Can you show me some of those 'mistakes?'" she questioned.

"Sure, there are tons of them," Jared quipped as he took a breath and started rolling with his attack. "First, there are two contradictory stories of Creation in Genesis chapters one and two. Next, the Bible says in one place that Judas hung himself, but in another place it says he fell into a field and his guts came out. Plus, in some places the Bible says God doesn't tempt people, but in other places it says he does tempt them. Add to that the fact that the Bible says that everything that God created was good, and yet the Bible says that God creates evil. Do I need to go on?" Jared said in a slightly condescending tone as he let the weight of his "contradictions" sink in.

Julianna was at a loss. She had always believed that the Bible was the Word of God, but in the face of so many "errors" she didn't have a clue where to start. She could do what so many Bible believers do—just wave off Jared's whole spiel with a "Well, whatever, I still believe the Bible is God's Word." That would be the easy way out. But failing to address Jared's accusations seemed to Julianna to be

cowardly and intellectually dishonest. She knew that the Bible says all Christians should be ready to give a defense to everyone who asks them about their beliefs. But how in the world was she supposed to deal with all that stuff Jared had thrown at her?

Of course, Julianna is not the first one to find herself in this position. It is often the case that skeptics, unbelievers, atheists, and infidels throw out so much dizzying information that Christians hardly know where to start. How can you productively approach such a situation as a Christian?

The first step is to take a deep breath and realize that there are no new atheistic arguments under the Sun. Everything that atheists are "preaching" right now has been said in one shape, form, or fashion before, and there is a logical, rational, intelligent answer to counter it. **Christianity is the only perfectly rational belief system**. It has nothing to fear from the most rigorous investigation. It has sustained the minds of many of the world's brightest and most critical thinkers for the last 2,000 years, and it will be around long after the modern generation of atheists is gone. Christianity has nothing to fear, and every allegation by atheism can be answered.

Second, one of the most effective tactics when dealing with atheists and unbelievers is to politely stop them and ask them to give you their strongest argument. Let us see how that might work in Jared's and Julianna's scenario.

After an initial shock, Julianna realized that Jared was spouting out so many accusations, there was no way she could answer them all. She waited for Jared to finish, and then said: "Jared, you know I can't answer all of those right now. In fact, for most of those you didn't even tell me what verses you were looking at. I'll tell you what, why don't you give me your strongest alleged contradiction and we can work through it together."

Now it was Jared's turn to be surprised. Most of the time, the Christians he used this list on were so stunned that they changed the subject, or refused to deal with the issues. This was the first time he had been challenged to consider which contradiction was the strongest. Instead of answering her question, he decided he'd try something else. "Well, there are just so many of them, and they are all so powerful, I've never thought about boiling it down to just one. Really there are hundreds."

Julianna refused to let up, "I know you say there are hundreds, but let's just work through one of them. We can't deal with 'hundreds' all at once. So if you would, just give me the one that is most convincing to you."

Again, Jared didn't really know what to say. He really hadn't done all that much research on each individual contradiction. He had been so impressed by how many there were, he hadn't worked through them in detail. In fact, come to think of it, he could not remember doing serious research on any single one. He knew he had read the same ones on different Internet sites and in the "big atheists'" books, and he figured they must be good if so many atheists repeated them. He decided he would just go with the one he had seen in the most books and on the most sites.

"Alright, what about how Judas died? The Bible says he hung himself, but it also says he fell into a field and his guts came out. That is a contradiction plain as day."

Let's press pause in our little dialogue and see what we are learning. Since there is no way to deal with every accusation at once, the only way to approach attacks like Jared's is to narrow down the discussion to one point at a

time. Furthermore, if you ask the unbeliever to give you his or her strongest single argument, if you can deal with it, you can certainly deal with all the weaker ones that the unbeliever will give you.

One of the most effective statements in any discussion is simply to say: "Will you please give me the single strongest argument you have against __________" (fill in the blank with whatever topic the unbeliever is talking about, such as "the Bible's inspiration," "Creation," or "the existence of God"). If the skeptic says something like, "My strongest argument against the Bible's inspiration is the fact that it is filled with contradictions." You then narrow the field again and say something like, "That is a great place to start. Can you give me the single most powerful alleged contradiction you know?"

By doing this, you are able to break the discussion into "bites" that you can handle. Once you do this, do not move on to the next point or argument until you have thoroughly dealt with the idea. What you will find often happens is that the atheist will attempt to give up on the one you are discussing and move on to the next argument. It will sound something like, "Well, yeah Judas might have been dead when his body fell into the field,[1] but what about God creating everything good and also creating evil?"[2] You see how quickly another allegation gets thrown in. Make sure that you insist on staying with one idea until you are both done with it.

When the skeptic finally does decide to leave that idea, it never hurts to politely remind him: "I asked you to provide me with your most powerful argument. You did and we have dealt with that. Before we move on to the next argument, I just want to point that out." Let me show you how this plays out in real life.

A while back a man (who we will call Jack) wrote the following e-mail to Apologetics Press about our *Discovery* Web site:

> While your website has been around for ten years, you are thousands of years behind on many of your answers. It's not so much that you haven't caught up to modern science, but in many instances you are dead wrong on your answers. Your website is absolutely horrible. It would be lovely if you could catch up to the 21st century.

We responded to Jack by saying:

> Thanks for writing. We appreciate feedback from our readers, even when it is negative. If you would not mind, would you please just provide **one example** of the "dead wrong" information that you have seen on the site? Thanks.

Notice that we were attempting to cut through his blanket statement about all our material being horrible by narrowing the discussion to one specific topic.

He responded: "When you quote the Bible for answers about the Universe and its history and to explain any type of phenomena, you are wrong."

Again, notice how hesitant he is to identify any real issue that could be nailed down and discussed. We wrote back: "Could you give us a 'for instance' of that? Thanks."

He wrote:

> From "Is Evolution Scientific?" [one of the articles on our site—KB]:
>
> "The question is: which idea, evolution or creation, is better supported by the facts? A careful study of this subject will show that 'creation' is much better supported than 'evolution' is."
>
> Why do public schools teach evolution if 'creation' is better supported by the facts?
>
> Also, evolution predicts that in the womb we produce gill sacs and a coat of fur which we shed before we are born. How does "creation" explain this phenomena?

At last, Jack is giving us something that is actually an issue that we can compare to the available evidence. We responded:

> Dear Jack,
>
> Thanks for writing. I appreciate the statement you have offered as evidence that we are wrong, and I appreciate your question about schools and your comment about gill sacs. Question, from 1912-1952 Piltdown man was used as evidence for evolution. We now know it was a fraud. Why would public schools have used it to teach evolution? Second, I think you will be more satisfied if you check this yourself, but I'll supply you with one article on it. Humans never have gill slits. That was a false idea based on evolution. See the following article http://www.answersingenesis.org/articles/2007/03/14/fishy-gill-slits. Actually, the idea of gill sacs or slits seems to me to make the creationist point clearly, that evolution is not confirmed by the evidence. Thanks for writing.

What did Jack have to say to this statement? He retorted: "You guys blow my mind. Have fun with you're [his use of the wrong "your"] theory." Jack never provided any evidence to support his allegation. When we did provide evidence that showed his accusation to be false, he had no response. By forcing Jack to provide a single idea or piece of evidence, we were able to cut through his attack and deal with it. Narrowing the discussion down to one idea is a great tactic to get at the truth of the issues being discussed.

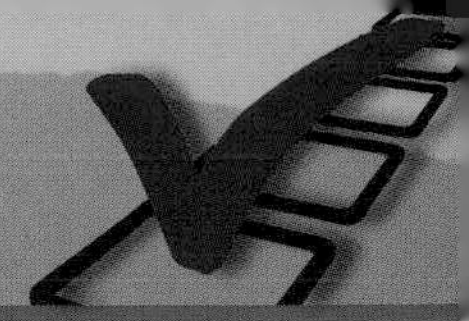

Chapter Notes

1. You can find the answer to this alleged contradiction on the Apologetics Press Web site in an article titled, "Did Judas Die Twice?" at the following Web address: http://www.apologeticspress.org/AllegedDiscrepancies.aspx?article=1761.
2. This claim is answered in an article on our site titled: "Does God Create 'Evil'?" It is written by Wayne Jackson and you can find it at this link: http://www.apologeticspress.org/APContent.aspx?category=11&article=1157.

Who Wants that Kind of Faith?

Some time ago, I was involved in a very productive discussion with two atheists. They were in their early thirties, intelligent, and extremely well spoken. We arranged a meeting at a local Mexican restaurant to discuss why they had chosen to adopt atheism, and reject God and Christianity. In the course of the two-hour discussion, it became clear that many of their complaints about "Christianity" were legitimate. In fact, I heartily agreed with many of their objections to "Christianity."

You will notice that I have put the term "Christianity" in quotation marks. That is because what they were calling Christianity was not true Christianity. Much of the "Christianity" that made the men so upset involved misrepresentations of God and misunderstandings of the Bible. For instance, during our talk, one of them explained that if John Calvin was right, and God picked some people to be saved and some to be lost, regardless of their choices, then God would be unjust. He explained this point in detail for several minutes. After listening to his refutation of Calvinism, I completely agreed with him. I then explained that Calvinism is not true Christianity. In his mind, Calvinism and Christianity were the same thing. He seemed very surprised that any "Christian" would agree that the idea of Calvinism is flawed.

By talking to a host of atheists, and reading the books and articles they produce, I have learned something very

important: most atheists in the country don't understand **New Testament Christianity**. They argue against "Christian" doctrines that have been made by men and are not biblical teachings from Christ at all. One excellent way to begin a discussion with an atheist is to make sure that you are both discussing the same "Christianity." Often the first place to begin is with the definition of faith.

A Wrong Definition of Faith

It is unfortunate for Christianity that some who call themselves Christians completely misunderstand the basic concept of faith. For many people, faith is a warm feeling in their hearts when they have failed to find evidence to justify their beliefs. Modern dictionaries have not helped to clear this up. In fact, they have included this idea in their definitions. For instance, *Webster's Ninth New Collegiate Dictionary* states that faith is "a firm belief in something for which **there is no proof.**" *The American Heritage Dictionary* published in 2000 gives as a primary definition of faith: "belief that does not rest on logical or material evidence."

The idea that faith is a warm, fuzzy feeling that does not require right thinking or evidence does not agree with what the Bible actually says about faith. The Christian philosopher Dick Sztanyo correctly noted: "There is not a single item in Christianity, upon which our souls' salvation depends, that is only 'probably' true. In each case, the evidence supplied is sufficient to establish conclusive proof regarding the truth of the Christian faith."[1]

The false view that faith is "a leap in the dark" without adequate evidence gives atheists plenty of ammunition to use against "Christianity." If believing in God is not established by rational, logical evidence, then we should

not believe in God. One famous atheist named Sam Harris wrote: "In fact, every religion preaches the truth of propositions for which no evidence is even *conceivable*."[2] He is wrong. But since many people who call themselves Christians teach that faith is not based on evidence, he thinks he is right.

Another famous atheist named Richard Dawkins said: "The whole point of religious faith, its strength and chief glory, is that it does not depend on rational justification."[3] Because of his belief that biblical faith is belief without rational justification, Dawkins concluded: "We believe in evolution because the evidence supports it, and we would abandon it overnight if new evidence arose to disprove it. No real fundamentalist would ever say anything like that."[4]

Dawkins would call any person who believes there is a God, and believes the Bible is God's Word, a "fundamentalist." What Dawkins really means to say is that no fundamentalist who has adopted the "popular" concept of faith would abandon his position if evidence were provided to the contrary. But if his definition of faith is wrong (which it is), then he is incorrect to say that those who believe in God would not change their views based on the evidence. In fact, according to a proper definition of biblical faith, **it is only because of correct thinking about the available evidence** that true Christians hold to their beliefs. A New Testament Christian can boldly state: "We believe in Christianity because the evidence supports it, and we would abandon it overnight if new evidence arose to disprove it."

When Dawkins stated, "Christianity, just as much as Islam, teaches children that unquestioned faith is a virtue. You don't have to make the case for what you believe,"[5] he showed his lack of knowledge of what biblical faith is.

Biblical faith is based on truth and reason, as the apostle Paul clearly stated in Acts 26:25. The prophet Isaiah emphasized this truth about biblical faith when He recorded God's invitation to the Israelites: "'Come now, and let us **reason together**,' says the Lord" (1:18). Luke, in his introduction to the book of Acts, pressed the point that Jesus' resurrection was attested by "many infallible proofs" (1:3). For one to believe in the resurrection requires faith **based on infallible proofs**.

Sam Harris wrote: "It is time that we admitted that faith is nothing more than the license religious people give one another to keep believing when reasons fail."[6] Harris' accusation is right when it is applied to false religions, and to those who attempt to defend Christianity without providing evidence for their belief. But his accusations cannot be used to attack true, biblical faith. Sadly, too many people who call themselves Christians open the door for the skeptical community to bash Christian "faith," when, in reality, the "faith" that is being destroyed was never biblical in the first place.

Let's Think About the Statement: "I Don't Have Enough Faith To Be An Atheist"

In the course of my work at Apologetics Press, I often hear Christians say, "Atheism is founded on so many unproven assumptions. It takes **more faith** to be an atheist than it does to be a Christian. I just don't have **enough faith** to be an atheist." This idea was expressed by Norman Geisler and Frank Turek in the title of their book *I Don't Have Enough Faith To Be An Atheist*. While I understand and appreciate the motivation behind this idea, we need to be careful about making such a statement. Here is why.

The false view that faith is "a leap in the dark" without adequate evidence is the concept that Christians have in mind when they say that it takes more faith to be an atheist than to be a Christian. According to a proper definition of biblical faith, however, it is only because of the evidence that true Christians hold their beliefs. **What it takes to be an atheist is not biblical faith.** To be an atheist, a person must choose to completely deny the concept of biblical faith and hold on to irrational ideas that have been **repeatedly disproven**.

Throughout the Bible, those who had great faith were commended,[7] and those who had little or no faith were sharply rebuked.[8] In fact, the Hebrews writer clearly stated that "without faith it is impossible to please Him [God], for he who comes to God must believe that He is, and that He is a rewarder of those who diligently seek Him."[9] Faith is a desirable trait by which a person thinks through the available evidence and comes to a proper conclusion based on that evidence. By allowing the religious world and the skeptical community to redefine faith as something negative, we have done a serious disservice to the biblical concept of faith.

If atheists had true faith, they should be commended for it; but they do not have faith. Instead, atheism is a **failure** to think about the evidence correctly and come to the right conclusion. It is the exact opposite of true faith. Romans 1:20 shows the contrast between biblical faith and atheism. That verse says: "For since the creation of the world His [God's] invisible attributes are clearly seen, being understood by the things that are made, even His eternal power and Godhead, so that they are without excuse." In this passage, faith means coming to the proper, rational conclusion that there is a God based on the evidence of

His creation. Irrational belief in spite of the evidence leads one to conclude there is no God. To arrive at this atheistic conclusion is to kick evidence, reason, and faith to the curb. Atheism uses improper reasoning supported only by subjective human whim—an approach that, sadly, will leave atheists "without excuse" on the Day of Judgment.

The idea of atheism is filled with error. It cannot account for the beginning of the Universe; it cannot give an adequate explanation for the obvious design in our world; atheism completely fails to offer a good explanation for human morality; and human freewill defies an atheistic explanation. To cling to atheism in the face of such overwhelming evidence takes an irrational belief that is motivated by something other than a sincere quest for truth and knowledge—it certainly is not true faith. So, in order to help the greater religious world and the skeptical community understand what true faith is, let's not misuse the word or attribute to atheism something it cannot rightly claim to have.

Conclusion

It is the sad truth that much of what is taught in the name of "Christianity" is not really what the Bible teaches. One reason some atheists are so confident in their unbelief is because ideas such as Calvinism and "blind faith" are so illogical and unreasonable. It is our job as Christians to defend true Christianity and to show the skeptical world the difference. When the Bible speaks of having faith, it does not discuss a faith that is a "leap in the dark," or "a firm belief based on unprovable assumptions." In fact, the biblical idea of faith is exactly the opposite. Biblical faith is a firm belief in that which can be documented as true.

Biblical faith says that we can **know** God exists,[10] we can **know** Jesus is His Son,[11] we can **know** the Bible is His Word,[12] and we can **know** how to be saved.[13] Faith is not a leap into the unknown, but is a firm commitment based on what is known.

NOTES

1. This quote is from his book *Faith and Reason*. The quote is on page 7. You can download his book from the A.P. Web site at this address: http://www.apologeticspress.org/pdfs/e-books_pdf/far.pdf.
2. This quote comes from Harris' book *The End of Faith* and is found on page 23.
3. From his book *God is Not Great*, p. 23.
4. *The God Delusion*, p. 283.
5. *The God Delusion*, p. 306.
6. *The End of Faith*, p. 67.
7. Luke 7:9
8. Matthew 8:26; Mark 16:14
9. Hebrews 11:6
10. Psalm 46:10
11. 1 John 5:20
12. 2 Peter 1:20-21
13. 1 John 5:13

Always Be Ready

[NOTE: This chapter, and the four that follow, are the most technical in the book. In my experience, I have learned that young people digest the atheistic arguments that are written in similar style quite readily. There is nothing in these chapters that I believe a discerning, diligent young person, who sincerely wants to know the truth on these matters, will find difficult to grasp.]

Are Atheists More Moral Than God?

In their zeal to convert people to atheism and away from a belief in God, atheists accuse God of being immoral. They claim that if God really is so good, why does He approve of murder, rape, slavery, racism, sexism, and a host of other immoral behaviors? They say that atheism provides a much better foundation for morality than the idea that there is some type of "invisible grandfather" in the sky waiting to reward and punish everybody.

Dan Barker and many of his fellow atheists claim that atheism offers the world a better system of morality than the one in the Bible. In fact, near the end of Dan's ten-minute rebuttal speech during our debate in 2009, he stated: "We can know that the atheistic way is actually a superior intellectual and moral way of thinking."[1] One primary reason Dan gave for his belief that the Bible's morality is flawed is that the Bible states that God has directly killed people, and that God has authorized others to kill people.

In Dan's discussion about Abraham's sacrifice of Isaac, Dan said that Abraham should not have been willing to obey God's command.

In his book *godless*, Barker said: "There is not enough space to mention all of the places in the bible where God committed, commanded or condoned murder."[2] In his *Letter to a Christian Nation*, Sam Harris wrote: "Anyone who believes that the Bible offers the best guidance we have on questions of morality has some very strange ideas about either guidance or morality."[3] In his landmark atheistic bestseller, *The God Delusion*, Richard Dawkins wrote the following as the opening paragraph of chapter two:

> The God of the Old Testament is arguably the most unpleasant character in all fiction: jealous and proud of it; a petty, unjust, unforgiving control-freak; a vindictive, bloodthirsty ethnic cleanser; a misogynistic, homophobic, racist, infanticidal, genocidal, filicidal, pestilential, megalomaniacal, sadomasochistic, capriciously malevolent bully.[4]

After listing several Old Testament verses pertaining to the conquest of Canaan, Dawkins referred to God as an "evil monster." Christopher Hitchens wrote that God's actions and instructions in the Old Testament had caused "the ground" to be "forever soaked with the blood of the innocent."[5]

Is it true that atheism offers a superior morality to that found in the Bible? Certainly not, but the first issue we need to discuss is the fact that atheism cannot even deal with the moral concepts of right or wrong.

Atheism Cannot Make "Moral" Judgments

The extreme irony of the atheistic argument is that atheism cannot even define the term "moral," much less use the concept against any other system. On February 12, 1998,

William Provine delivered a speech on the campus of the University of Tennessee. In a summary of that speech, his introductory comments are recorded in the following words: "Naturalistic evolution has clear consequences that Charles Darwin understood perfectly. 1) No gods worth having exist; 2) no life after death exists; 3) **no ultimate foundation for ethics exists**; 4) no ultimate meaning in life exists; and 5) human free will is nonexistent."[6] It is clear from Provine's comments that he believes naturalistic evolution has no way to produce an "ultimate foundation for ethics."

If atheism is true and humans evolved from non-living slime, then any sense of morals must simply be caused by the physical working of the brain. In theory, atheistic scientists and philosophers admit this truth. Charles Darwin understood it perfectly. He wrote: "A man who has no assured and ever present belief in the existence of a personal God or of a future existence with retribution and reward, can have for his rule of life, as far as I can see, only to follow those **impulses and instincts** which are the strongest or which seem to him the best ones."[7] Dan Barker admitted this in his debate with Peter Payne, when he stated: "There are no actions in and of themselves that are always absolutely right or wrong. It depends on the context. You cannot name an action that is always absolutely right or wrong. I can think of an exception in any case."[8]

If there is no moral standard other than human "impulses and instincts," then any attempt to accuse another person (or God) of immoral behavior boils down to nothing more than one person not liking the way another person does things. While the atheist may claim not to like God's actions, he cannot say God is "wrong." If he did, that

would show there is a moral standard. If actions can be labeled as truly moral or immoral, then atheism cannot be correct. As C.S. Lewis rightly stated:

> My argument against God was that the universe seemed so cruel and unjust. But how had I got this idea of *just* and *unjust*? A man does not call a line crooked unless he has some idea of a straight line. What was I comparing this universe with when I called it unjust...? Of course, I could have given up my idea of justice by saying it was nothing but a private idea of my own. But if I did that, then my argument against God collapsed too—for the argument depended on saying that the world was really unjust, not simply that it did not happen to please my private fancies. Thus in the very act of trying to prove that God did not exist—in other words, that the whole of reality was senseless—I found I was forced to assume that one part of reality—namely my idea of justice—was full of sense. Consequently, atheism turns out to be too simple.[9]

If there truly are cases of justice and injustice, then God must exist. Furthermore, we will show that the God of the Bible never is unjust in His dealings with humanity. On the contrary, the atheistic position finds itself mired in injustice at every turn.

Dan Barker and Rape

I understand that even discussing the term rape in a book for teens is a little risky, but you need to understand where atheistic "morality" leads. If there is no foundation for deciding exactly what is right and wrong, then any action could be argued to be right **under certain circumstances**. That is exactly what we see the atheists being forced to admit. In 2009, during the debate I had with Dan Barker, he confessed that atheism could be used to justify any

actions. I asked him if atheism could be used to say that it could be right to rape a person. He said that if raping one girl would save all of humanity, then it would be the right thing to do. I then asked him if, according to atheism, it would be right to rape two girls to save all humanity. He said yes. I asked if it would be right to rape 2,000 girls. He said yes. I asked if it would be right to rape two million. He said it would be his moral obligation to rape them to save the lives of all the rest of humankind.[10]

Thus, we see that atheism can be used to justify the most immoral actions. And we see that atheists have absolutely no possible way to accuse God of immorality. If there really is a right and wrong, then atheism is false and God wins the day. Atheism cannot even discuss morality, much less claim a **superior** morality to that of the God of the Bible.

Having said that, in the following four chapters we will deal with some of the most common attacks from the atheistic community against the morality of God. In each section we will show their attacks to be wrong. But just remember, as we go through these attacks, atheism cannot really even discuss such matters if "there are no actions in and of themselves that are always absolutely right or wrong. It depends on the context."

CHAPTER NOTES

1. To watch the entire debate, you can go to: http://www.apologeticspress.org/MediaPlayer.aspx?media=3639.
2. *Godless*, p. 177.
3. *Letter To a Christian Nation*, p. 14.
4. *The God Delusion*, p. 31.
5. *God Is Not Great*, p. 107.
6. You can find a summary of William Provine's speech titled, "Evolution: Free Will and Punishment and Meaning in Life," at the following Web address: http://eeb.bio.utk.edu/darwin/DarwinDayProvineAddress.htm.
7. That statement is found on page 94 of Charles Darwin's autobiography.
8. Dan Barker debated Peter Payne in 2005 on the campus of the University of Wisconsin. The debate was titled, "Does Ethics Require God?" You can find the audio files of the lesson at this link: http://ffrf.org/legacy/about/bybarker/ethics_debate.php.
9. This quote is taken from C.S. Lewis' book *Mere Christianity*. It is found on pages 45-46 in the edition published by Simon and Schuster in 1952.
10. You can find a brief video which contains that segment of the debate at http://www.youtube.com/watch?v=oFwrq1pNF0o.

Is God Immoral for Killing Innocent Children? [Part 1]

Many modern atheists accuse God of being immoral. One of the main reasons for this is the Bible says God is responsible for killing people (this comes mostly from the Old Testament). Supposedly, since God has killed people, or commanded them to be killed, then He must be immoral. Generally, the atheistic argument against God begins with blanket statements about all of God's actions that caused anyone to die. When the case is pressed, however, the atheistic argument must be immediately qualified. Even atheists are forced to admit **some** killing might be justified.

Could it be that some of God's actions were against people who had committed crimes worthy of death? Atheist Sam Harris noted that he believes that the mere holding of certain beliefs could be a good enough cause for putting some people to death.[1] Almost all atheists admit that certain actions, such as serial killing, theft, or child abuse, deserve to be punished in **some** way. They do not all agree with Harris that the death penalty is right, but they would argue that some type of punishment is acceptable.

Once the atheistic community admits that people who break certain laws should be punished, the only question left to decide is **how** should they be punished. Atheists are forced to admit that justice and the concept of punishment answer their accusations against God killing some people.

At this point the atheist is forced to change his argument to discuss only innocent people.

The argument changes from, "God is immoral because He has killed people," to "God is immoral because He has killed **innocent** people." Since human infants are rightly viewed by atheists as innocent, the argument is then restated as "God is immoral because He has killed innocent human infants." Dan Barker summarized this argument well in his debate with Peter Payne. In his remarks concerning God's commandment in Numbers 31 for Moses to destroy the Midianites, he stated: "Maybe some of those men were guilty of committing war crimes. And maybe some of them were justifiably guilty, Peter, of committing some kind of crimes. **But the children? The fetuses?**"[2]

It is important to note, then, that a large number of the instances where God caused someone's death were examples of divine punishment of adults who were "justifiably guilty" of punishable crimes. For instance, Moses listed several perverse practices that the Israelites were told to avoid. He stated: "Do not defile yourselves with any of these things; for by all these the nations are defiled, which I am casting out before you. For the land is defiled; therefore I visit the **punishment of its iniquity** upon it, and the land vomits out its inhabitants."[3]

Having said that, it must also be recognized that not all the people God has killed have been guilty of such crimes. It is true that the Bible records several stories in which God caused the death of innocent children: the Flood,[4] the death of the first born in Egypt,[5] the annihilation of the Midianites,[6] the death of the Amalekites,[7] etc. Using these instances, atheists claim that God cannot be moral because He kills **innocent** children. The atheists then

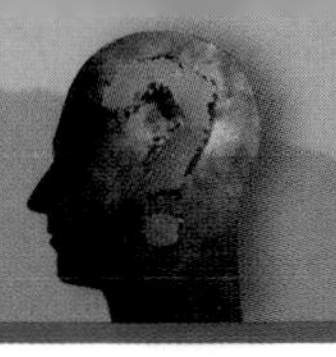

insist that modern-day atheism would never approve of such, and atheism is morally superior to belief in God.

Atheism Has No problem Killing Innocent Children

A closer look at atheistic morality, however, quickly shows that atheists do not believe that it is morally wrong to kill **all** innocent children. According to the atheistic community, abortion is viewed as moral. Dan Barker said that abortion is a "blessing."[8] One line of reasoning used by atheists to justify the practice is the idea that humans should not be treated differently than animals, since humans are nothing more than animals. They say that the fact that an embryo is "human" is no reason to give it special status. Richard Dawkins wrote: "An early embryo has the sentience, as well as the semblance, of a tadpole."[9]

Atheist Sam Harris noted: "If you are concerned about suffering in this universe, killing a fly should present you with greater moral difficulties than killing a human blastocyst [three-day-old human embryo—KB]."[10] He further stated: "If you are worried about human suffering, abortion should rank very low on your list of concerns."[11] Many in the atheistic community argue that unborn humans are not real "persons," and killing them is not the same as killing a person. Sam Harris wrote: "Many of us consider human fetuses in the first trimester to be **more or less like rabbits**."[12] James Rachels stated:

> Some unfortunate humans—perhaps because they have suffered brain damage—are not rational agents. What are we to say about them? The natural conclusion, according to the doctrine we are considering, would be that their status is that of mere animals. And perhaps we should go on to

> conclude that they may be used as non-human animals are used—perhaps as laboratory subjects, **or as food**.[13]

Isn't it ironic that Barker protested that God could not cause the death of an unborn human "fetus" and still be considered moral, and yet the bulk of the atheistic community says that those fetuses are the moral equivalent of rabbits? How can the atheist accuse God of immorality, and claim to have a superior morality, when the atheist has no moral problem killing babies?

In response, God's accusers attempt to make a difference between a "fetus" in its mother's womb, and a child already born. That distinction has been demolished by one of their own. Peter Singer, the man Dan Barker calls the world's leading ethicist, admits that an unborn child and one that is born are the same. Does this force him to the conclusion that abortion should be stopped? No. On the contrary, he believes we should be able to kill children that are already born!

In his chapter titled "Justifying Infanticide," Singer concluded that human infants are "replaceable." What does Singer mean by "replaceable"? He pointed out that if a mother has decided that she will have two children, and the second child is born with hemophilia, then that infant can be disposed of and replaced by another child. He argued that this would not violate any moral code of ethics. He explained: "Therefore, if killing the hemophiliac infant has no adverse effect on others, it would, according to the total view, be right to kill him. The total view treats **infants** as replaceable."[14]

He went on to argue that many in society would be horrified at killing an infant with a disability like hemophilia, but without good reason—according to his view.

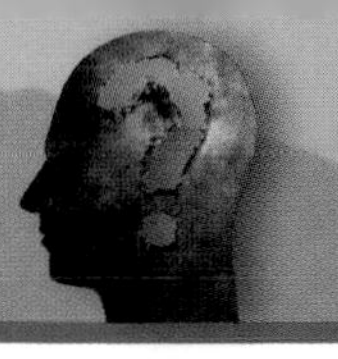

He argued that such is done regularly before birth, when a mother aborts an unborn child. He stated:

> When death occurs before birth, replaceability does not conflict with generally accepted moral convictions. That a fetus is known to be disabled is widely accepted as a ground for abortion. Yet in discussing abortion, we say **that birth does not mark a morally significant dividing line**. I cannot see how one could defend the view that fetuses may be "replaced" before birth, but newborn infants may not.[15]

Singer went on to say that parents should be given a certain amount of time after a child is born to decide whether or not they would like to kill the child. He wrote: "If disabled newborn infants were not regarded as having a right to life until, say, a week or a month after birth it would allow parents, in consultation with their doctors, to choose on the basis of far greater knowledge of the infant's condition than is possible before birth."[16] One has to wonder why Singer would stop at one week or one month. Why not simply say that it is morally right for parents to kill their infants at one year or five years? Singer concluded his chapter on infant killing with these words: "Nevertheless the main point is clear: **killing a disabled infant is not morally equivalent to killing a person**. Very often it is **not wrong at all.**"[17]

It is clear, then, that atheism does not have moral problems killing all innocent babies, only those innocent babies that they consider "worthy" to live. How in the world would a person make a moral judgment about which children were "worthy to live?" Singer, Harris, and others say that a child's mental capability, physical disability, or other criteria should be used to arrive at the answer. Dan Barker has given his opinion about how to make such moral decisions. He claimed that "morality is simply acting with the intention to minimize harm." He said the way

to avoid making mistakes in ethical judgments is to "be as informed as possible about the likely consequences of the actions being considered."[18]

Using Barker's thinking, if God knows everything, then only God would be in the best position to know all the consequences of killing infants. Could it be that all the infants born to the Amalekites had diseases, or were infected with an STD that was passed to them from their mothers? Could it be that the firstborn children in Egypt, or infants in the Flood, had some type of brain damage, terminal cancer, hemophilia, etc.? The atheistic community cannot accuse God of immorally killing infants and children when the atheists themselves say that some infant killing is good.

Once again, the atheistic argument must be changed. The argument has moved from: "God is immoral because He killed people," to "God is immoral because He killed innocent babies," to "God is immoral because He killed innocent babies that **we atheists feel** should have lived." Ultimately, then, the atheistic position is arguing that atheists, not God, should be the ones who decide when the death of an innocent child is acceptable.

Atheism Takes "All That There Is" From Innocent Children

As with most false belief systems, atheism's arguments often double back on themselves. Supposedly, God is immoral for killing innocent children. Yet atheists believe the death of certain innocent children is acceptable. Have we then simply arrived at the point where both atheistic and theistic morality are equally moral or immoral? Certainly not.

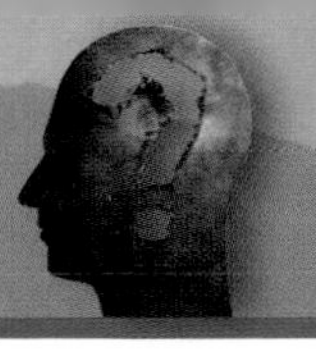

One major difference between the atheistic position and the biblical position is what is at stake with the loss of physical life. According to atheism, this physical life is all that any living organism has. Dan Barker stated: "Since **this is the only life we atheists have**, each decision is crucial and we are accountable for our actions right now."[19] He went on to say that life "is dear. It is fleeting. It is vibrant and vulnerable. It is heart breaking. It can be lost. It will be lost. But we exist now. We are caring, intelligent animals and can treasure our brief lives."

Since Dan and his fellow atheists do not believe in the soul or any type of afterlife, this brief, physical existence is the sum total of a person's life. If that is the case, when Barker, Harris, Singer, and others advocate killing innocent babies, in their minds, they are taking from those babies all that they have—the entirety of their existence. They have set themselves up as the Sovereign court that has the right to take life from their fellow humans, which they believe to be **everything** a human has. If any position is immoral, the atheistic position is. The biblical view, however, can be shown to possess no such immorality.

Physical Life is not "All There Is"

Atheism has trapped itself in the position of stating that the death of innocent children can be moral, even if that death results in the loss of everything that child has. Yet the biblical position does not fall into the same moral trap as atheism, because it recognizes the truth that physical life is not all there is. The Bible recognizes life as a privilege that can be revoked by God, the Giver of life. It also states the fact that death is not complete loss, and in many cases can actually benefit the one who dies.

The Bible explains that every person has a soul that will live forever, long after physical life on this Earth is over.[20] The Bible stresses the fact that the immortal soul of each person is of much more value than that person's physical life on this Earth. Jesus Christ said: "For what profit is it to a man if he gains the whole world, and loses his own soul? Or what will a man give in exchange for his soul?"[21]

Although the skeptic might object, and claim that an answer from the Bible is not acceptable, such an objection falls flat for one primary reason: the skeptic used the Bible to formulate his argument. Where do we learn that the Lord killed babies? From the Bible. Where should we look for an answer to this issue? The answer should be: the Bible. If the problem is formulated from the Bible, then the Bible should be given the opportunity to explain itself. As long as the skeptic uses the Bible to formulate the problem, we certainly can use the Bible to solve the problem. One primary aspect of the biblical solution is that every human has an immortal soul that will exist long after this physical life is over.

[Continued in Next Chapter]

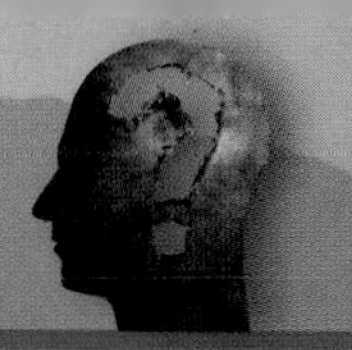

CHAPTER NOTES

1. This is from Harris' book *The End of Faith*, on pp. 52-53.
2. Dan Barker and Peter Payne debate, March 14, 2005 at the University of Wisconsin.
3. Leviticus 18:24-25
4. Genesis 7
5. Exodus 12:29-30
6. Numbers 31
7. 1 Samuel 15
8. Dan Barker debated John Rankin on May 5, 2006 in Plymouth, MA. For more information on Barker's position, see his book *Losing Faith in Faith*, pp. 135 and 213.
9. *The God Delusion*, p. 297.
10. *Letter to a Christian Nation*, p. 30.
11. *Letter to a Christian Nation*, p. 37.
12. *The End of Faith*, p. 177.
13. *Created from Animals: The Moral Implications of Darwinism*, p. 186.
14. *Writings on an Ethical Life*, p. 190. Peter Singer made similar comments in an article titled, "Sanctity of Life, Quality of Life," that was printed in 1983 in *Pediatrics*, volume 72, number 1, pp. 128-129.
15. *Writings on an Ethical Life*, p. 191.
16. *Writings on an Ethical Life*, p. 193.
17. *Writings on an Ethical Life*, p. 193.
18. *Godless*, p. 214.
19. *Godless*, p. 215.
20. Matthew 25:46
21. Matthew 16:26

Is God Immoral for Killing Innocent Children? [Part 2][1]

Physical Death is Not Necessarily Bad

With the value of the soul in mind, let us examine several verses that prove that physical death is not necessarily evil. In a letter to the Philippians, the apostle Paul wrote from prison to encourage the Christians in the city of Philippi. He included some very important comments about the way he and God viewed death. In Philippians 1:21-23, Paul wrote: "For to me, to live is Christ, and to **die is gain**. But if I live on in the flesh, this will mean fruit from my labor; yet what I shall choose I cannot tell. For I am hard pressed between the two, having a desire **to depart** and be with Christ, **which is far better.**" Paul, a faithful Christian, said that death was a welcome visitor. In fact, Paul said that the end of his physical life on this Earth would be "far better" than living. For Paul, as well as for any faithful Christian, the end of physical life is not loss, but gain. Such would apply to innocent children as well, since they are in a safe condition and go to paradise when they die.[2]

Other verses in the Bible show that the loss of physical life is not necessarily bad. The prophet Isaiah wrote: "The righteous perishes, and no man takes it to heart; merciful

men are taken away, while no one considers that the righteous **is taken away from evil**. **He shall enter into peace**; they shall rest in their beds, each one walking in his uprightness."[3] Isaiah recognized that people would view the death of the righteous incorrectly. Since most people are only thinking about this physical life, they misunderstand the death of the righteous. For people who are in a right relationship with the Creator, death takes them away from a world filled with sin and gives them rest in eternity.

The psalmist wrote, "Precious in the sight of the Lord is the death of His saints."[4] Death is not always bad. In fact, the Bible shows that death can be great gain in which a righteous person is taken away from evil and allowed to enter peace and rest. God looks upon the death of His faithful followers as precious. Skeptics who charge God with wickedness because He has ended the **physical** lives of innocent babies are wrong. They refuse to recognize the reality of the immortal soul. Instead of the death of innocent children being an evil thing, it is often a blessing for that child to be taken away from a life of hardship and taken into paradise. In order for a skeptic to charge God with cruelty, the skeptic must prove that there is no immortal soul, and that physical life is the only reality—which the skeptic cannot prove. Failure to accept the reality of the soul and the spiritual realm will always result in an incorrect view of the nature of God. "The righteous perishes… while no one considers that the righteous is taken away from evil."

We could ask who is moral: the atheist who has no problem approving of the death of innocent children, thinking that he is taking from them the only life they have? Or an

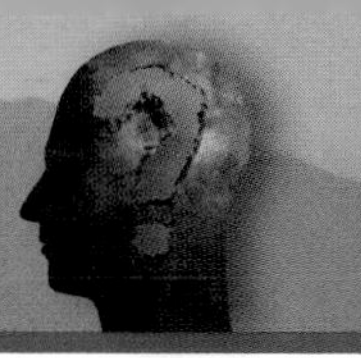

all-knowing God Who takes back the physical life He gave the child, exchanging it for an eternal life of happiness?

Why Not Kill All the Christians and Babies?

Atheists are forced to admit that their beliefs permit the killing of some babies. And they are forced to admit that **if** there is an afterlife, then the biblical description of God's activities could be moral. But at this point, atheists shift the argument in a last ditch effort to save face. If death can be, and sometimes is, better for the innocent child or for the Christian, why not kill all children and execute all Christians as soon as they come up out of the waters of baptism?[5] The atheist contends that if we say that death can be a better situation for some, then this position implies that we should kill every person that death would benefit.

Before dealing with this new argument, it should be noted that we have laid the other to rest. We have shown that it is impossible for atheism to accuse God of immorality in his dealings with innocent children. Since atheism's attack against God's character has failed on that front, the maneuver is changed to accuse the follower of God of not carrying his belief to its "end" by killing all those who would benefit. One reason that atheists make this point is because many of them believe that humans have the right to kill those who they see as "expendable." Of course, atheism does not base this judgment on the idea that certain **babies** or other **innocent people** would benefit, but that **society** would benefit. Here again, notice that God is supposed to be immoral because He "sinned" against innocent children by taking their lives, yet atheism cares nothing for innocent children, but claims to care for the society.

In truth, atheism implies that once a certain group of people, whether unborn babies, hemophiliacs, or brain-damaged adults, is thought to be "expendable," then humans have the moral right, and sometimes obligation, to get rid of them. The atheist berates the Christian for not taking his beliefs far enough (in the atheist's opinion). If certain people would benefit from death, then the atheist contends we should be willing to kill everyone who would benefit. If we are not willing to do this, then the atheist demands that our belief involves a moral absurdity. Yet, the fact that death is beneficial to some cannot be used to say we have the **right** to kill all those that **we think** it would benefit.

What Humans Do Not Know

One very important reason humans cannot kill all those people who we think might benefit from death is because we do not know all the consequences of such actions. Remember that Dan Barker stated that the way to make moral decisions is to "try to be as informed as possible about the likely consequences of the actions being considered."[6] Could it be that human judgments about who has the right to live or die would be flawed based on limited knowledge of the consequences? Certainly. Suppose the hemophiliac child that Singer said could be killed possessed the mind that would have discovered the cure for cancer. Or what if the brain-damaged patient that the atheistic community determines could be destroyed was going to make a remarkable recovery if he had been allowed to live?

Once again, the Christian could simply argue that God is the only one in the position to authorize death, since only God knows all the consequences. The atheistic community might attempt to protest that God does not know

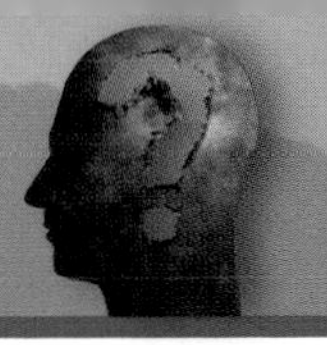

everything. But atheism is completely helpless to argue against the idea that **if** God knows everything, then only He is in the position to make the truly moral decision. Using Barker's reasoning, when God's actions do not agree with those advocated by atheists, God can simply answer them by saying, "What you don't know is...."

Also, there is no possible way that humans can know all the good things that might be done by the Christians and children that live, even though death would be better for them personally. The apostle Paul alluded to this fact when he said that it was better for him to die and be with the Lord, but it was more needful to the other Christians for him to stay alive and help them.[7] Books could not contain the countless good works, hospitals, orphanages, soup kitchens, humanitarian programs, and educational ventures that have been undertaken by Christians. It is important to understand that a strong Christian example is one of the most valuable tools that God uses to bring others to Him. Jesus said that when Christians are following His teachings, others see their good works and glorify God.[8] Furthermore, the lives of children offer the world examples of purity and innocence that are worth copying.[9] While it is true that death can be a better situation for Christians and children, it is also true that their lives provide a leavening effect on all human society. Only God is in a position to understand all the ways a child's life can affect the world.

Ownership and Authorization

The mere fact that only God knows all consequences is sufficient to establish that He is the only authority in matters of human life and death. Yet, His omniscience is not the only attribute that puts Him in the final position

of authority. The fact that all physical life originates with God gives Him the right to decide when and how that life should be maintained. In speaking of human death, the writer of Ecclesiastes stated: "Then the dust will return to the earth as it was, and the spirit will return **to God who gave it**."[10] The apostle Paul boldly declared to the pagan Athenians that in God "we live and move and have our being."[11] If God gives life to all humans, then only He has the right to say when that life has accomplished its purpose, or under what circumstances life may be taken.

In addition to the fact that God gives life and, has the authority to take it, He also has the power to give it back if He chooses. Throughout the Bible we read of instances in which God chose to give life back to those who were dead, the most thoroughly documented example of that being the resurrection of Jesus Christ.[12]

In fact, Abraham alluded to this fact during his preparations to sacrifice Isaac. After traveling close to the place appointed for the sacrifice, Abraham left his servants some distance from the mountain, and said to them: "Stay here with the donkey; the lad and I will go yonder and worship, and **we** will come back to you."[13] Notice that Abraham used the plural pronoun "we," indicating that both he and Isaac would return. The New Testament gives additional insight into Abraham's thinking. In Hebrews 11:17-19, the text states: "By faith Abraham, when he was tested, offered up Isaac, and he who had received the promises offered up his only begotten...accounting that **God was able to raise him up, even from the dead**...." Abraham knew that God had promised to bless him with many descendants who would come from Isaac. He was willing to sacrifice him because he knew God would raise him from the dead and fulfill His promise. Therefore, Abraham

knew that if he did kill Isaac, it would be temporary and his son would live again. Since God gives physical life to all, and since He can raise people from the dead whenever He chooses, then any accusation of injustice that fails to take these facts into view cannot be legitimate.

Conclusion

It is evident that atheism has no grounds upon which to attack God's character. Atheists contend that a loving God should not kill innocent babies. But those same atheists say that killing innocent babies could be a blessing under "the right" circumstances. Atheists contend that God is immoral for taking the lives of innocent children. Yet the atheist believes that it is permissible to take the lives of innocent children, even when doing so means that those children are being robbed of their entire existence. Yet, according to the biblical view, those children are being spared a life of pain and misery and ushered into a life of eternal happiness.

Atheism contends that its adherents are in a position to determine which children should live and die, and yet the knowledge of the consequences of such decisions goes far beyond their human ability. Only an all-knowing God could see all the consequences involved. The atheist contends that human life can be taken by other humans based solely on reasoning about benefits to society and other human opinions. The biblical position shows that God is the Giver of life, and only He has the authority to decide when that life has accomplished its purpose. In reality, the atheistic view proves to be the truly immoral position.

Chapter Notes

1. This chapter picks up immediately where the last one left off without any introduction.
2. I have written an article titled, "Do Babies Go to Hell When They Die?" You can find it on the Apologetics Press Web site at the following link: http://www.apologeticspress.org/apcontent.aspx?category=13&article=1201.
3. Isaiah 57:1-2
4. Psalm 116:15
5. For a good discussion on how to be saved, you can read the small booklet that Eric Lyons and I co-wrote. It is titled, *Receiving the Gift of Salvation*. You can download it free from the A.P. Web site at this link: http://www.apologeticspress.org/pdfs/e-books_pdf/Receiving%20the%20Gift%20of%20Salvation.pdf.
6. *Godless*, p. 214.
7. Philippians 1:22-25
8. Matthew 5:13-16
9. Matthew 18:1-5
10. Ecclesiastes 12:7
11. Acts 17:28
12. I have written an in-depth article on Jesus' resurrection titled, "Jesus Christ—Dead or Alive?" You can find it on the A.P. Web site at: http://www.apologeticspress.org/articles/121.
13. Genesis 22:5

The Bible and Slavery

For years, atheists have attacked the Bible. Many of them insist that since the God of the Bible is pro-slavery, then He is immoral. They contend that any book or person that does not condemn all slavery is immoral. For instance, atheist Sam Harris said:

> Consider the question of slavery. The entire civilized world now agrees that slavery is an abomination. What moral instruction do we get from the God of Abraham on this subject? Consult the Bible and you will discover that the creator of the universe clearly expects us to keep slaves.... Nothing in Christian theology remedies the appalling deficiencies of the Bible on what is perhaps the greatest—and the *easiest*—moral question our society has ever had to face.[1]

Dan Barker stated:

> Why did Jesus, the unrivaled moral example, never once speak out against slavery? Why did the loving, wise Son of God forget to mention that human bondage is a brutal institution? Why did he incorporate it into his teachings, as if it were the most natural thing in the world? I'll tell you why: because he supported it. The Old Testament endorses and encourages slavery, and Jesus, being equal to God, supposedly wrote the old laws, so he *had* to support slavery.[2]

The accusation made by atheists is easy to understand. "The Bible does not condemn all forms of slavery, thus

the Bible and the God of the Bible are immoral." What can we say to such an accusation?

If Humans Evolved...

First, we must remember that atheism does not have any room to say that something is immoral. Remember that atheism implies that there are no moral absolutes. Darwin said that without a belief in God, people follow the instincts and impulses that seem best to them. What if a person follows his instinct to enslave another person? How can the atheistic community say that is morally wrong?

In fact, if humans evolved from primordial slime, what difference does it make if one human forces another to be a slave? What if making humans slaves would help the human species evolve better (not that evolution is even possible, but I'm just using it as an illustration)? When we look at the animal kingdom, we see that some animals and insects make slaves of other organisms. For instance, there is a type of ant known as the Amazonian Slave Making Ant that forces other kinds of ants into slavery. Would the atheists claim that such ants are acting immorally? They would not. But if humans evolved just as these ants, then how can atheists contend that forcing another human into slavery is wrong, if a person is following the instincts and impulses which seem best? In fact, if evolution were true and only the strongest survive, wouldn't it help evolution for the strongest to enslave the weaker? As I'm sure you can see, atheism simply cannot say slavery is morally wrong.

What Everyone Knows about Some Types of Slavery

Second, the atheists that are attacking God make a blanket statement that all slavery is bad. Yet they are forced to admit that not **all** slavery is wrong. They admit that some types of slavery could be morally right. For instance, when a man in the United States is convicted of murder, he often is sentenced to life in prison. During his life sentence, he is forced by the State to do (or not do) certain things. He is justly confined to a small living space, and his freedoms are taken away. Sometimes, he is compelled by the State to work long hours, for which he does not receive even minimum wage.

Would it be justifiable to label his loss of freedom as a type of slavery? Yes, it would. However, is his loss of freedom morally wrong? Certainly not. He has become a slave of the State, because he violated certain laws that were designed to ensure the liberty of his fellow citizen, whom he murdered. Therefore, we can see that slavery is not **necessarily** wrong.

Taking that into account, we must also ask: Who has the right to determine when slavery can be imposed on a certain person or group of people? The answer, of course, is God. In the Old Testament, immoral nations who practiced unspeakable evils surrounded the Hebrews. In order to rid the world of their destructive influence, the children of Israel dealt with them in several ways. One of those ways included forcing them to become slaves. Many of the slave regulations in the Old Testament deal with the treatment of these wicked people. They were allowed to live, but they were subjected to slavery, much like a lifetime prison sentence in modern criminal cases.

Also, Israelites that were convicted of crimes could be made slaves as well. In Exodus 22:1-3, the Bible discusses the situation in which a thief was caught in the act of stealing. The thief was instructed to restore what he stole, returning four sheep for every one stolen and five oxen for every one stolen. The text states, "He should make full restitution; if he has nothing, then he shall be sold for his theft."[3] Being sold into slavery was often a government regulated punishment based on a criminal action—which is basically what the prison system in the United States is today.

The Bible is Not Racist

It is very important to understand that the slavery regulated in the Bible had absolutely nothing to do with race, color, or ethnic background. Certain nations, as a whole, were captured and enslaved because of their wicked, idolatrous practices. But it is not true that they were enslaved because they were thought to be an inferior race. Leviticus 19:34 states: "But the stranger who dwells among you shall be to you as one born among you, and you shall love him as yourself; for you were strangers in the land of Egypt: I am the Lord your God." Deuteronomy 24:14 reads: "You shall not oppress a hired servant who is poor and needy, whether one of your brethren, or one of the aliens [strangers—KB] who is in your land within your gates."

The New Testament stresses the idea that every human soul is equally valuable. Galatians 3:28 says: "There is neither Jew nor Greek, there is neither slave nor free, there is neither male nor female; for you are all one man in Christ Jesus." The idea that one nation or race is superior to another does not come from the Bible. Racism, like

that displayed by many during the period of slavery in the United States, has always been a sin.[4]

What the Atheist Must Do…But Cannot

In order for the atheist to rightly accuse the Bible of being immoral concerning slavery, he must show that the Bible approves of immoral, unjust human behavior. But the atheist cannot do this. In fact, the atheist is forced to admit that some types of slavery, like that found in prisons, are justifiable. Therefore, if the Bible were to make a statement that condemns all forms of slavery, then the Bible would be crippling governments, taking from them legitimate ways of dealing with criminal behavior.

Christianity Abolishes Slavery

If everyone were to follow the teachings of Jesus and His inspired apostles, there would be no cruel slavery in the world. Slavery would have been nonexistent if everyone from the first century forward had adhered to Jesus' admonition in Matthew 7:12: "Therefore, whatever you want men to do to you, do also to them." There would be no slavery if all people would obey the words of Peter: "Finally, all of you be of one mind, having compassion for one another, love as brothers, be tenderhearted, be courteous."[5] Truly, the teachings of the Lord and the apostles would have abolished slavery like no other social reform system ever known.

Conclusion

It has been established that certain types of "slavery" are morally acceptable and not wrong. The prison system in the United States shows that slavery (such as when a criminal becomes a "slave" of the state) not only is permissible, but sometimes necessary. In order for the biblical stance on slavery to be unjust, it must be determined that the specific rules about slavery described in the text are immoral and unfair. However, the biblical stance on slavery is perfectly in line with true justice. All regulations found in the Bible were established for the just treatment of everyone involved. God's instructions about slavery have a clear ring of justice, compassion, mercy, and kindness. When analyzed fairly and fully, the idea of slavery gives the honest person one more piece of evidence that points to the perfection of the God of the Bible.[6]

Chapter Notes

1. *Letter to a Christian Nation*, pp. 14 and 18.
2. *Godless*, p. 178.
3. Exodus 22:3
4. Read Acts 17:26-31. Also, it is interesting to note that Charles Darwin recognized that evolution actually does imply racism. Eric Lyons and I have written an article titled: "Darwin, Evolution, and Racism." You can find it on the A.P. Web site at: http://www.apologeticspress.org/apcontent.aspx?category=9&article=2654.
5. 1 Peter 3:8
6. For a more in-depth discussion of this topic see my article titled: "Defending the Bible's Position on Slavery." It is on the A.P. Web site at this link: http://www.apologeticspress.org/apcontent.aspx?category=11&article=1587.

The Bible and Women

Many best-selling books by famous atheists are filled with accusations against God. Atheists often claim that they reject the Bible because of, among other things, the way the Bible treats women. According to these unbelievers, the Bible writers viewed women as inferior creatures who are less valuable than men and do not deserve to be treated with respect and dignity.

Preacher-turned-atheist, Charles Templeton, summarized this view well when he wrote, "The Bible is a book by and for men. The women in it are secondary creatures and usually inferior."[1] In his book, *The God Delusion*, renowned atheist Richard Dawkins stated that the God of the Bible is "misogynistic" (a word that means "hating women").[2] Dan Barker made a similar assertion when he wrote: "Although the bible is neither antiabortion nor pro-family, it does provide modern antiabortionists with a biblical basis for the *real* motivation behind their views: the bible is not pro-life, but it is anti-woman. A patriarchal system cannot stand women who are free."[3] Famed skeptic Christopher Hitchens wrote:

> A consistent proof that religion is man-made and anthropomorphic can also be found in the fact that it is usually "man" made, in the sense of masculine, as well.... The Old Testament, as Christians condescendingly call it, has woman cloned from man for his use and comfort. The

> New Testament has Saint Paul expressing both fear and contempt for the female.[4]

Is it true that the biblical treatment of women is immoral? Not in any way. On the contrary, just the opposite is the case. The Bible's treatment of women is in perfect agreement with truth and correct moral teaching.

Women and Evolution

Atheistic evolution is plagued by numerous problems regarding morality. In fact, we have already seen that atheism cannot answer questions about good and evil, right and wrong. Only belief in a supernatural Creator provides a foundation for human morality. Therefore, any attempt to question the morality of the God of the Bible based on atheistic ideas will fail.

Furthermore, while the Bible does not state that men are superior to women, evolution actually does. In his monumental work, *The Descent of Man*, Charles Darwin wrote:

> The chief distinction in the intellectual powers of the two sexes is shown by man's attaining to a **higher eminence, in whatever he takes up, than can woman**—whether requiring deep thought, reason, or imagination, or merely the use of the senses and hands.... [T]he average of **mental power in man must be above that of woman**.... **[M]an has ultimately become superior to woman.**[5]

According to Darwin, males had evolved to a higher level than females. As evidence of his conclusion, he simply stated that males "attain to a higher eminence" in everything that they take up when compared to females.

Using this way of thinking, it would be impossible to condemn men for treating women as inferior. If men have the mental or physical ability to treat women as inferior, it must mean that men are stronger or more fit to survive. It

is ironic that the atheistic community, that is so enamored with Darwin, is suggesting that the Bible's view of women is immoral. In reality, if their view of atheistic evolution is true, then all male-dominated societies are that way because males are more able to dominate. And since survival of the fittest is desired, then one must conclude that a male dominated society, in which women are viewed as inferior to men (as Darwin put it), must be the natural order of things. In truth, those who hold to atheism have a much more thorny problem with their ideas as they relate to women than those who believe in the Bible.

The Value of Women According to the Bible

Atheist Charles Templeton wrote concerning the Bible: "Women were associated with evil and weakness. Indeed, Israelite males sometimes thanked God in the synagogue that they had not been born women."[6] Upon closer inspection, it becomes clear that both the Old and New Testaments show that women are equally as valuable as men. While it is the case that the Bible presents **different roles** for men and women, it is not the case that men are **valued** more than women.

Wisdom as the Portrait of a Woman

The book of Proverbs is known as wisdom literature, because the main theme of the book is the concept of wisdom. The writer stated: "Wisdom is the principal thing; therefore get wisdom."[7] To stress the importance of wisdom, he wrote: "For wisdom is better than rubies, and all the things one may desire cannot be compared with

her."[8] The Bible writers viewed wisdom as a personality trait that is extremely valuable.

What picture was used to personify this valuable trait? Throughout the book of Proverbs, the idea of wisdom is pictured as a woman. The text reads: "Wisdom has built **her** house;"[9] "Does not wisdom cry out, and understanding lift up **her** voice? **She** takes **her** stand on the top of the high hill."[10] The best picture of wisdom that the Proverbs writer could paint was that of a woman.[11] Needless to say, you do not hear these passages that glorify woman being quoted by most atheists.

God's Attitude Illustrated with Traits of a Woman

While it is true that God does not have a specific gender as humans do,[12] the Bible sometimes illustrates some of His traits by comparing them to traits possessed by certain people. For instance, the God of the Bible often compares the love that He has for humans with the love that a father has for his children.[13] If the God of the Bible were truly sexist, then the Bible would never compare any of His traits to those possessed by women.

Yet the Bible records instances in which the God of heaven compares His traits to similar traits found in women. For instance, John Willis noted: "A most compelling piece of evidence that OT writers had a high regard for women is that they describe God as a mother."[14] Willis then mentioned at least three passages as examples, including Isaiah 66:12: "For thus says the Lord.... As one whom his mother comforts, so I will comfort you; and you shall be comforted in Jerusalem."

Women Made in the Image of God

Many skeptics claim that the creation of Eve from Adam's rib to be a helper for man shows that woman is viewed in the Bible as less valuable or inferior to man. Recall the claim of Hitchens when he wrote: "The Old Testament... has woman cloned from man for his use and comfort."[15] Supposedly, the fact that Eve was Adam's helper somehow "proves" she is less important.

There are at least two problems with this thinking. First, it completely ignores the stress that the Bible places on women being made in God's image **exactly like man**. Genesis 1:27 states: "So God created man in His own image; in the image of God He created him, **male and female** he created them." Contrary to many religious groups and sexist thinkers (like Darwin), the Bible insists that both male and female were made in God's image. Both deserve to be treated with dignity.

So what of the word "helper"? Is it true that a "helper" implies that the person she helps is superior or of greater worth? That simply cannot be the case. In John 15:26, Jesus explained that the Holy Spirit was going to visit the apostles after His resurrection. He stated: "But when the Helper comes, whom I will send to you from the Father, the Spirit of truth who proceeds from the Father, He will testify of Me." Using the skeptic's reasoning, we would be forced to conclude that the Holy Spirit is inferior to the apostles, since He is referred to as "the Helper." Such a conclusion is obviously absurd. Furthermore, Jesus Christ Himself stated that He came into this world not "to be served, but to serve."[16] Would that mean that since He was "serving" or "helping" mankind, then He was inferior

in some way to humans? Certainly not. The concept of "helping" or "serving" carries no meaning of inferiority.

Galatians 3:28—The Golden Text of Equality

The apostle Paul is often demonized as a woman-hater who feared the opposite sex and held them in contempt. Remember that Charles Templeton said: "To judge by his epistles, the apostle Paul was a confirmed misogynist."[17] Such statements conveniently overlook one of the boldest statements of gender and race equality in all ancient religious literature. In Galatians 3:28, Paul wrote: "There is neither Jew nor Greek, there is neither slave nor free, there is neither **male nor female**; for you are all one in Christ Jesus." Paul clearly wrote that men and women are of the same spiritual value.

Different Jobs, Not Different Value

So why do some say that Paul hated women, even with Galatians 3:28 in view? The main reason for this is that Paul wrote that men and women have been given different duties and roles. The skeptical community mistakenly equates the idea of **different roles**, with the idea of **different status**. As Templeton wrote: "In his first letter to the church at Corinth, Paul states unequivocally that men and women have a different **status** before God."[18] Supposedly, since Paul instructs men to be elders,[19] and to lead publically in worship,[20] and husbands to be the "head" of their homes,[21] then he must view women as less able, less valuable, or inferior to men.[22]

Is it true that since the Bible gives men and women different roles, their status or worth must be unequal? Certainly not. In Titus 3:1, Paul explained that Christians were supposed to be subject to rulers and authorities and obey the government.[23] From that statement, is it correct to conclude that Paul views all those in governmental positions to be of more value than Christians? Does this passage imply that, because Christians are to obey other humans who are in governmental positions, Paul sees those in governmental positions as mentally, physically, or spiritually superior to Christians? Not in any way. The mere fact that Christians are to obey those in the government says nothing about the spiritual status or value of either party. It only addresses different roles that each person plays.

Again, in 1 Timothy 6:2, Paul instructs Christian servants to be obedient to their own masters. Does this imply that Paul believed masters to be superior, or to be of more worth than servants? No. It simply shows a difference in roles, not status.

Furthermore, while skeptics are quick to attack Paul's ordination of men as elders and leaders in their homes, those skeptics neglect to include the responsibilities involved in such roles. Husbands are called upon to give their lives for their wives,[24] to physically provide food, shelter, and clothing for their families,[25] and to love their wives as much as they love themselves.[26]

While much is said about the "unfairness" of Paul's instructions, it is productive to ask who would get the last spot on a life boat if a Christian husband and wife were on a sinking ship? The Christian husband gives himself for his wife in such instances. Is that fair that he is called upon to accept the sacrificial role of giving himself for his wife? Is

she more valuable than he is because God calls upon him to protect her, cherish her, and die for her if necessary? Does God consider women more valuable, and therefore, more important to keep alive than men? No. It is simply a difference in assigned roles, not in status or worth.

Conclusion

Outspoken atheists claim that the Bible presents a sexist picture of men and women. Supposedly, God and the Bible writers place more value on men, and view women as inferior and of less value. This accusation falls apart, however, when all of the Bible is considered. Careful study shows that the Bible writers personified attributes such as wisdom in the form of a woman. God himself compares traits that He possesses to similar traits found in women. Both the Old and New Testaments are filled with stories about the actions of faithful, powerful women such as Deborah, Mary, Esther, Ruth, Anna, and Huldah.

The apostle Paul, who is often accused of hating women, makes one of the boldest statements of gender equality ever recorded in religious literature. Furthermore, it is clear that the different roles Paul discussed for men and women do not show either gender to be superior. In truth, the Bible presents the clearest picture of gender equality, value, and worth ever recorded in either ancient or modern literature. The status of women in the Holy Scriptures is not a challenge to its divine inspiration. On the contrary, the biblical treatment of women actually provides another piece of evidence for the Bible's perfection and inspiration.

CHAPTER NOTES

1. *Farewell to God*, p. 177.
2. *The God Delusion*, p. 131.
3. *Losing Faith in Faith*, p. 212.
4. *God is not Great*, p. 54.
5. This quote can be found in the 1871 version of *The Descent of Man*, on pp. 873-874.
6. *Farewell to God*, p. 184.
7. Proverbs 3:7
8. Proverbs 8:11
9. Proverbs 9:1
10. Proverbs 8:1-2
11. John Willis has some good things to say that were very helpful to me on page 37 of his chapter titled "Women in the Old Testament." That chapter is a part of a book titled *Essays in Early Christianity*, Volume 1.
12. You can read more about that in an article titled "Is God Male?" It is on the A.P. Web site at: http://www.apologeticspress.org/articles/162.
13. 1 John 3:1-2
14. "Women in the Old Testament," pp. 37-39.
15. *God is not Great*, p. 54.
16. Mark 10:45.
17. *Farewell to God*, p. 185.
18. *Farewell to God*, p. 186.
19. Titus 1:5-9
20. 1 Corinthians 14:34-35 and 1 Timothy 2:8-15
21. Ephesians 5:22-24
22. Wayne Jackson has an excellent article on the roles of men and women as they relate to the verses mentioned in this chapter. You can find it on his *Christian Courier* Web site at the following address: http://www.christiancourier.com/articles/169-womans-role-in-the-church.
23. See also Romans 13.
24. Ephesians 5:25
25. 1 Timothy 5:8
26. Ephesians 5:25

Evil, Pain, and Suffering

John sat on the end of his bed with his head buried deeply in his hands. His face was red, tear-stained, and puffy from several days of ceaseless crying. The past few days all seemed to run together, but he could remember quite well how it all started. Jennifer, his lovely girlfriend for the past three years, was sitting in the passenger seat talking about the movie they had just watched. Suddenly, the headlights in the other lane swerved in front of John's car. He slammed on the breaks and began to turn the steering wheel hard to the left. When he did, the oncoming car crashed into the passenger's side. John made it out of the wreck with only a few cuts and scratches, and so did the drunk who caused the accident, but Jennifer was rushed to the hospital. After several hours of surgery, a nervous-looking doctor walked into the small room where John was waiting. "Are you John Smith?" he asked. "Yes, I am," replied John. "How is she?" The doctor took him by the arm, looked him in the eye, and said: "I'm terribly sorry, but your girlfriend has died. We tried our best, but there was nothing more we could do."

Now, as John sat on his bed, two weeks after Jennifer's death, questions raged in his mind. Jennifer had always been very religious; she went to church twice on Sundays, and every Wednesday night for Bible study. She was heavily involved with the "meals on wheels" program, and even talked John into going to Peru last year to take part in a

door-knocking campaign. Why did God let her die? Why didn't the Lord take the drunk driver who had caused the accident, or the drug dealer on the other side of town? Why Jennifer? John just kept thinking, "If God is so kind and loving, and if He is all-powerful, why does He allow innocent people to suffer and die?"

John came face-to-face with a problem that practically every person eventually encounters: If there is an all-powerful God, and if He is all-good, then why do bad things happen to innocent people? Many people have abandoned their belief in God because of the presence of suffering in their lives or in the lives of those close to them. Some have lost children, others have uttered what they feel are unanswered prayers, and still others have seen their very best friends tragically taken from them. Faced with these terrible events, they have decided that there is no God.

Without God There is No Evil

Before proceeding further, it is necessary to define more precisely what the "problem of evil, pain, and suffering" is. When skeptics and atheists talk about "the problem of evil," they mean that the Bible describes God as a God of love.[1] In addition, the Bible repeatedly states that God is all-powerful[2] and can accomplish anything He desires.[3] Thus, those unbelievers who propose the "problem of evil" argue that if God is a loving being, He would not allow evil, pain, and suffering to exist on the Earth. Since evil, pain, and suffering do exist, then the skeptic demands that God does not exist. Or, says the skeptic, if God does exist, He is not all-powerful and cannot stop the evil. Or if He is all-powerful, He must not be loving, since He allows people to suffer. Thus, the unbeliever argues that the loving, all-powerful God of the Bible cannot exist.

Supposedly, the "problem of evil" presents an unanswerable problem for the Christian. We will show, however, that the "problem of evil" is a much bigger problem for the atheist than it is for the Christian theist. As we have discussed in previous chapters, if we were to seek a definition of "evil" from atheism, we would soon realize there is not one. It is impossible for atheism to label anything as "evil" or "good." Atheism says that there are no moral absolutes, so how would atheism be able to define evil? In fact, if we could prove that some actions are actually evil, that would prove there are moral absolutes, and that would prove that there is a God. Theistic apologist, William Lane Craig, has summarized the issue quite well. He stated:

> I think that evil, paradoxically, actually proves the existence of God. My argument would go like this: If God does not exist then objective moral values do not exist. (2) Evil exists, (3) therefore objective moral values exist, that is to say, some things are really evil. Therefore, God exists. Thus, although evil and suffering at one level seem to call into question God's existence, on a deeper more fundamental level, they actually prove God's existence.[4]

Why Does God Allow Suffering?

Let's continue to answer this question by making it clear that the Word of God must be used as the main source in this discussion; after all, both the problem and the solution can be found within its pages. Think with me. Where does the idea originate that God is all-powerful? The idea comes straight from passages of the Bible such as Genesis 17:1 where God said, "I am Almighty God," or Matthew 19:26 where Jesus said, "With men this is impossible, but

with God all things are possible." And the same principle applies to the idea that God is all-loving.[5]

Unfortunately, when we appeal to the Bible for an answer to the problem of evil, pain, and suffering, some people object. They say that we should not use the Bible; but they do not realize that **they** used the Bible to formulate the problem. After all, if the Bible did not teach that God is all-loving and all-powerful, then this problem would not exist in the first place. Therefore, we can and must use the Bible to find the solution to the problem.

After God had finished creating everything, it was "very good."[6] However, Adam and Eve sinned against God, and, as a result, brought pain and suffering into the world. God has always given human beings the right to make their own decisions. He did not create us as robots that have no choice. In Psalm 32:9, King David wrote: "Do not be like the horse or like the mule, which have no understanding, which must be harnessed with bit and bridle, else they will not come near you." God never has forced (and never will force) humans to obey Him. He does not want us to be like the horse or mule that must be forced into His service. Instead, He graciously allows humans to make their own decisions. Much of the suffering present in the world today is a direct result of the misuse of the freedom of choice of past generations. Paul wrote in Romans 5:18: "Therefore, as through one man's offense judgment came to all men." Mankind—not God—is to blame for the suffering in this world.

But do not think that **all** the pain and suffering in this world can be blamed on past generations. Each one of us makes wrong decisions and incorrect judgments by which we bring pain upon ourselves and upon others. The young man who decides to "sow his wild oats" eventually will learn that every person reaps what he sows.[7]

Many destitute people have awakened in a gutter because they freely chose to get drunk the night before. Many teenage girls have become pregnant outside of marriage due to poor decisions and lack of will power. And many drunk drivers have killed themselves, their passengers, and innocent victims, because they would not give up the keys.

As young people, you must understand that all of your actions have consequences. What you do today determines what your life will be like tomorrow. God will allow you to be forgiven of your sins, but He will not always remove the painful consequences of your actions. Much of the pain and suffering that we experience in this world is our own fault.

In addition, God created a world ruled by natural laws. If a man steps off the roof of the Empire State Building, gravity will pull him to the pavement beneath. If a boy steps in front of a moving freight train, the momentum of the train most likely will kill the child. All of nature is regulated by natural laws set in place by God. They are the same for everyone (believer and unbeliever alike). In Luke 13:2-5, Jesus told the story of 18 people who died when the tower of Siloam fell on them. Did they die because they were more wicked or more deserving of death than others around them? No, they died because of natural laws that were in effect. Fortunately, natural laws are constant so that we can study them and benefit from them. We are not left to sort out some kind of random system that works one day but not the next.

Furthermore, there are times when suffering is beneficial. Think of the man whose chest begins to throb as he begins to have a heart attack, or the woman whose side starts to ache at the onset of appendicitis. Pain often sends us to

the doctor for prevention or cure. Also, tragedy can help humans develop some of the most treasured traits known to mankind—bravery, heroism, and self-sacrifice—all of which flourish in less-than-perfect circumstances. Yet those who exhibit such qualities are said to go "above and beyond the call of duty." Wasn't that the point Christ was making in John 15:13 when He said, "Greater love has no one than this, than to lay down one's life for his friends"?

But sometimes there seems to be no logical explanation for the immense suffering that a person is experiencing. Take the Old Testament character of Job as an example. He lost 10 children and all of his wealth in a few short hours. Yet the Bible describes him as upright and righteous. Why would God allow such a man to suffer? James 1:2-3 helps us see the answer: "My brethren, count it all joy when you fall into various trials, knowing that the testing of your faith produces patience." Jesus Christ was the only truly innocent man ever to live, yet He suffered immensely. The fact is, pain and suffering have benefits that we sometimes cannot see. But God knows what will be better for us in the long run.

Conclusion

Each one of us will come face to face with the problem of evil and suffering in our own lives. We have seen that atheism cannot explain the idea of evil. There can only be evil in a world created by God. Furthermore, we understand that some of the pain in our lives is caused by our own freedom to choose. At other times, our pain may be caused by others, or those of previous generations. In addition, we live in an orderly world governed by natural laws. This situation sometimes brings about suffering, but it also allows humans to study the world and understand how it works. It is also true that pain can be used to build character and bring about things that are far more valuable than a pain-free life.

Instead of blaming God for pain or denying His existence, we should look to Him for strength and let tragedies remind us that this world was never intended to be our final home.[8] James 4:14 reminds us that our time on this Earth is extremely brief. The fact that even the Son of God was subjected to terrible evil, pain, and suffering[9] proves that God loves and cares for His creation. He could have abandoned us to our own sinful devices, but instead, "God demonstrates His own love toward us, in that while we were still sinners, Christ died for us."[10]

The evil, pain, or suffering that an unbeliever endures is difficult to understand at times, but it is not the greatest tragedy of his life. The greatest tragedy of the unbeliever's life—for now and for eternity—is his unwillingness to accept the love of God.

CHAPTER NOTES

1. 1 John 4:8
2. Genesis 17:1
3. Job 42:2 and Matthew 19:26
4. William Lane Craig has a brief video on YouTube explaining this at the following address: http://www.youtube.com/watch?v=8ZTG5xyefEo.
5. 1 John 4:8,16
6. Genesis 1:31
7. Galatians 6:7
8. Read Hebrews 11:13-16.
9. Read Hebrews 5:8 and 1 Peter 2:21-25.
10. Romans 5:8

Can a Loving God Send People to an Eternal Hell?

Just the word "hell" brings to mind the most vivid and terrifying pictures. Most children learn at an early age about the "bad place" where the devil and wicked people will burn…forever. Because of the horrible nature of hell, many people have a problem believing that a loving God would send anyone there. In fact, the idea of hell has driven some people away from the Bible and God. Here is one of the major arguments against hell, the Bible, and God:

- The Bible teaches that God is love.
- A loving God would not punish people forever in a place like hell.
- Therefore, there must not be a hell, or God must not be a loving God, or the Bible must be wrong.

What Does the Bible Teach?

It would be extremely difficult for a person to read the Bible and miss the fact that it describes God as a loving and caring Creator. In 1 John 4:7-8, the writer declares that love comes from God and that "God is love." Throughout the Scriptures, God's love for His creatures is repeated time and time again.

On the other hand, it is equally clear that the Bible teaches that there is a very real place of torment called hell. Jesus

often talked about such a place. For instance, in Matthew 25:41 Jesus said: "Then He will also say to those on the left hand, 'Depart from Me, you cursed, into the everlasting fire prepared for the devil and his angels.'" He repeatedly stressed that hell would be a place of everlasting torment: "And these will go away into everlasting punishment, but the righteous into eternal life."[1]

We can see that the Bible plainly describes God as a loving Creator, yet it still tells of an eternal place of punishment. So, how can both statements be true?

The Nature of Love

What does the Bible mean when it says that God is love? In today's society, the concept of love is often misunderstood. Many people today think that a loving person is one who always tries to keep others out of every pain or discomfort. Punishment is often looked upon as an "unloving" thing to do. But that is not the case. In fact, a loving person often will cause some pain to others in order to accomplish a greater good. For instance, suppose a mother tells her four-year-old son to stop putting the hairdryer into his little sister's bath water, but the child continues his mischievous and dangerous activity? That child will most likely be punished. Maybe he will get a swift swat on the leg or have to sit in a corner. The pain or discomfort inflicted on the child is for his own good and the good of his sister. His mother loves her children and wants what is best for them.

We can see, then, that a loving person could inflict some pain upon another person in order to accomplish a greater good. But the problem still remains that atheists say that eternal punishment seems to be too harsh and permanent

to come from a loving God. It is at this point that the justice of God must be considered.

What is Justice?

God is not a one-sided Being. He has many different attributes that need to be considered. One of those attributes is love, but another is justice. Psalm 89:14 states that "righteousness and justice" are the foundation of God's throne. What is justice? Justice is the principle that everyone gets what he or she "deserves." It is not difficult to recognize justice. Suppose a certain judge in a large U.S. city let every murderer walk away from his courtroom without any punishment. Even though many of the murderers had killed several people in cold blood, imagine the judge waving his hand, patting the murderer on the shoulder, and saying something like, "I am feeling very generous and loving today, so you are free to go without any punishment." The judge obviously would not be administering justice, and he should promptly be relieved of his position. In the same way, if God did not provide a way to deal with and punish the sinful actions that we humans commit, then justice could not be the foundation of His throne.[2]

If You Do the Crime, You've Got to Do the Time

Another thing that everyone recognizes about justice is the fact that the punishment often lasts longer than the crime. For example, suppose a man walks into a bank with a .45 caliber pistol, shoots two tellers, and robs the bank. Later, he is arrested, tried, and found guilty. The

punishment for such actions almost always lasts longer than the crime. The actual shooting and looting might have taken only three minutes to accomplish, but the criminal will pay for those three minutes with the remainder of his life in prison.

Justice frequently demands that punishment last longer than the crime. Those who contend that hell will not be eternal say that forever is "too long" to punish someone. But once a person concedes that, according to justice, punishment lasts longer than the crime (and all rational people must concede this point), then it is merely a matter of deciding how long punishment should be. And since God is the "righteous judge" Who knows the hearts and minds of all men, it makes sense that He alone should be the One to decide how long punishment should last.

Furthermore, this "too long" argument goes both ways. I dare say none of us would stand at the gates of heaven and refuse to go in because we think that the rewards are "too great" and will last "too long." The truth of the matter is, the Lord created every human being as an immortal soul. Whatever we do in this life has eternal consequences. When we sin, that sin "sticks" to our soul for eternity, unless we accept God's plan to wash away those sins.

God—The Righteous Judge and Ruler

God created this world and the humans who live here; therefore, He knows exactly what should and should not be done in order to ensure that everyone has an opportunity to be with Him in heaven. Abraham once described God as "the Judge of all the earth."[3] God is the only Being capable of creating, sustaining, and judging the world. The prophet Isaiah said that God's thoughts are higher

than man's thoughts, and His ways are higher than man's ways.[4] And the apostle Paul said that the "foolishness of God is wiser than men."[5]

A first-grader can see the fact that God is "smarter" than men. Has man ever been able to create a living person from a pile of dirt? Can man control the weather, or cause the seasons to change? Do humans have the power to make planets orbit the Sun, or control gravity? Of course, the answer to all these questions is "No!" Man cannot do the things that God can do, and man does not know all the things that God knows. Therefore, when a human says that "a loving God would not punish people for eternity," but God's Word says that even though God is love, He will punish the wicked for eternity, who is in a better position to make the call? That is like asking who is in a better position to call a baseball player out at first base—the umpire two feet away from the play, or the fan who is sitting 200 feet up in the bleachers in the "nose-bleed" section who was helping his child tie her shoe during the play? The truth is, once a person recognizes the fact that there is a Creator, he or she must also recognize the fact that the Creator is in total control of His creation.

Love and Justice—Together at Last

Because God is love, He wants to save all mankind from an eternity in hell. But because He is also just, He must make sure that sin receives a proper punishment—like any good judge must do. Therefore He devised a plan to accomplish His goal of saving mankind. By sending Jesus to die on the cross for humanity, "He made Him who knew no sin to be sin for us."[6] The torture and death of Christ allowed God to remain just and yet still save sinful men.

Isaiah described this situation many years before Christ even came to the Earth when the prophet said: "He was wounded for our transgressions, He was bruised for our iniquities; the chastisement for our peace was upon Him, and by His stripes we are healed."[7]

Conclusion—God Won't Twist Your Arm

True love always allows people to make their own decisions. And God will not **force** anyone to accept Christ. Those who reject Christ, and do not obey the Gospel, do not have the debt of their sins washed away by His cleansing blood. Therefore, according to the principle of justice, they must pay for their sins with their own souls.

Since God is love, He has given humans every possible chance to repent and be saved from hell. But the truth of the matter is, some people will never be obedient to God no matter how many chances they are given.

In Revelation 16:9, the Bible tells of a group of wicked men who suffered greatly, yet "they did not repent and give Him the glory." It is reported that the secular writer Robert Ingersoll said, "If there is a God who would damn his children forever, I would rather go to hell than go to heaven."[8] Atheist Dan Barker boldly declared: "Speaking for myself, if the biblical heaven and hell exist, **I would choose hell.**"[9] C.S. Lewis insightfully noted: "There are only two kinds of people in the end: those who say to God, 'Thy will be done,' and those to whom God says, in the end, '*Thy* will be done.' All that are in Hell, choose it."[10] Timothy Keller added: "All God does in the end with people is give them what they most want, including freedom from himself. What could be more fair than that?"[11]

The concept of hell at first may seem "hard to swallow," but it does not contradict the infinite love and justice of the heavenly Father. The Bible tells us plainly that God will cast people into hell forever **who choose** to go there; make the choice not to be one of them.

CHAPTER NOTES

1. Matthew 25:46
2. The outline for this chapter came from a sermon done by Wayne Jackson many years ago titled: "The Goodness of God and an Eternal Hell."
3. Genesis 18:25
4. Isaiah 55:9
5. 1 Corinthians 1:25
6. 2 Corinthians 5:21
7. Isaiah 53:5
8. http://en.wikipedia.org/wiki/User:Rnelson.
9. *Godless*, p. 170.
10. That quote comes from C.S. Lewis' book *The Great Divorce*, p. 72.
11. *The Reason for God*, p. 79.

Chapter 12

"Creation is Untestable"

The atheistic community is aggressively trying to discredit all belief in a supernatural Creator. To do that, atheists often spread pamphlets, write books, and post videos that argue against God. Their materials generally repeat common arguments in favor of atheism, evolution, and other incorrect ideas. One common argument used by atheists against the concept of God and creation is the idea that creation is untestable.

Atheists claim that the creation of the Universe is not "scientific" because such a supernatural Creator cannot be tested using scientific instruments and procedures. Eugenie Scott, the Executive Director of the National Center for Science Education, evolutionist and outspoken opponent of creation, has expressed this idea: "The ultimate statement of creationism—that the present universe came about as the result of the action or actions of a divine Creator—is thus outside the abilities of science to test."[1] Supposedly, because God cannot be "controlled" in an experiment, and because He is a supernatural, non-physical Being, then any information that involves such a God cannot be "scientific."

It is interesting to note, however, that Scott makes some very important admissions when it comes to the ways scientists gather data and formulate their theories. In her discussion of data collection, she said that some scientific facts are gathered from indirect observation. She stated:

> In some fields, not only is it impossible to directly control the variables, but the phenomena themselves may not be directly observable. A research design known as *indirect experimentation* is often utilized in such fields. Explanations can be tested **even if the phenomena being studied are too far away, too small, or too far back in time to be observed directly.** For example, giant planets recently have been discovered orbiting distant stars—though we cannot directly observe them.[2]

She proceeded to say that because we know that large planets would have quite a large gravitational pull, and because we see the distant stars "wobble" like they have been pulled by planet gravitation, then we can know that "these planetary giants do exist," and even estimate their sizes.

Let's analyze what Ms. Scott is suggesting: (1) there are some things in this world that we cannot observe directly; (2) we cannot do tests or experiments on the actual object; (3) nor can we see, taste, hear, smell, or touch them. But we can **know** that they exist due to the fact that we can see their effects on things.

One reason Scott is forced to admit the legitimacy of indirect observation is the fact that evolution cannot be tested directly. She admits: "Indeed, no paleontologist has ever observed one species evolving into another, but as we have seen, a theory can be scientific even if its phenomena are not directly observable."[3] According to Scott, we cannot observe evolution in action, but we can look at the effects it has left in the fossil record and other areas and call it a "scientific" discipline.

It may come as quite a surprise to the reader that Ms. Scott's explanation of indirect experimentation is almost identical to the evidence given by the apostle Paul for the existence of God: "For since the creation of the world His

invisible attributes are clearly seen, being understood by the things which are made, even His eternal power and Godhead, so that they are without excuse."[4] Paul was simply saying that the general population cannot directly observe the Creator, and yet the effects the Creator causes in this observable Universe are so directly tied to His power that those who refuse to recognize His existence are without excuse.

Can we look into this Universe and see complex biological machinery that demands a mind? Yes. Can we look at the qualities of matter and know that matter cannot be eternal and must have had a starting point? Absolutely. Is it possible to locate systems in nature that could not have evolved, but must have been designed by an Intelligence that far surpasses any and all human intelligence? Certainly. Then just as surely as Ms. Scott recognizes that much scientific data comes from indirect observation, a rational thinker must admit the possibility and legitimacy of getting information about the Creator in the same way.

If we can look at phenomena that we know must be caused by a mind, such as computers, cars, and houses, then we can study the characteristics that show they were caused by a mind and look for those same characteristics in nature. When we do, we find abundant evidence that a Mind must have been involved in the Universe to bring about the effects that we observe directly. In truth, Creation is the most rational, scientific explanation for the material Universe we see.

Chapter Notes

1. *Evolution vs. Creationism: An Introduction*, p. 19.
2. *Evolution vs. Creationism: An Introduction*, p. 6.
3. *Evolution vs. Creationism: An Introduction*, p. 14.
4. Romans 1:20

Chapter 13

"All Religion Is Bad Because Some Is"

In a debate, a "straw man" is a weak, illogical position that is easily refuted. The more powerful, true position is then coupled with the straw man, and both are said to fall together. But the stronger position never actually is refuted by the opposition. For example, suppose a person stated that he owned a congenial, safe dog. The man's neighbor argued that such was impossible. The opposing neighbor then told a story about a family's pet pitbull that went berserk and killed someone. Then he stated that this incident proves that all pets are dangerous. Does his argument follow from the evidence? Of course not. He might have proven that one family's pitbull was dangerous, but he did not prove that all pets are dangerous. In fact, it would be easy to multiply numerous examples of dangerous pets, but proving those specific pets to be dangerous could not be applied to all pets.

This idea must be understood when reading modern atheistic writings that claim to prove that the ideas of God and religion are harmful to society. Their argument, in a nutshell, goes like this: Since we can list examples of "bad" religions and religious fanatics that were (or are) harmful to society, then all religions or ideas about God are harmful to society.

Just so you don't think that I'm constructing a straw man, let us consult the writings of a very popular, militant atheist, the late Christopher Hitchens. Hitchens has been

critically acclaimed as "one of the most prolific, as well as brilliant, journalists of our time" according to the *London Observer*. The *Los Angeles Times* stated that he is a "political and literary journalist extraordinaire." In secular circles, then, it must be admitted that this man was no slouch.

One of Hitchens' most popular books is titled *God Is Not Great: How Religion Poisons Everything*. Notice that his subtitle is broad enough to lump all religions into it: Islam, New Testament Christianity, Catholicism, Hinduism, Buddhism, etc. Hitchens then proceeded, in the pages of his book, to list many horrible things that people have done in the name of "religion." He said: "Religion has caused innumerable people not just to conduct themselves no better than others, but to award themselves permission to behave in ways that would make a brothel-keeper or an ethnic cleanser raise an eyebrow."[1] Hitchens even titled chapter two of his book, "Religion Kills." In it he wrote: "Here, then, is a very brief summary of the religiously inspired cruelty I witnessed…."[2] He then recounted horror stories of several evil things done in the name of "religion." Furthermore, Hitchens stated: "If one comprehends the fallacies of any 'revealed' religion, one comprehends them all."[3]

Can Hitchens and others document atrocities performed in the name of religion? Of course they can. Does this prove that all religion is false and that if a person can spot a flaw in one religion, then he has disproved the validity of all religions? Absolutely not. Can you imagine what would happen if this type of argument were used in other areas of life? Apply such thinking to food. Many foods are poisonous and kill people, thus all foods should be avoided. Apply it to electricity. Many people have died while using electricity, thus all electrical use is bad for society. Or apply it to activities like swimming. Many have drowned

while swimming, thus all swimming leads to drowning and should be avoided. What if it were applied to surgery? Since it is true that thousands of people have died during surgery, or as a result of surgery, then all surgery should be avoided because it leads to death. Obviously, the incorrect idea that **all** religion is harmful to society, because it can be proven that **some** religions are harmful, should be quickly discarded by any honest, thoughtful observer.

The existence of God and the truthfulness of New Testament Christianity do not stand or fall based on how true or false other religions are. In fact, Hitchens and others are right in the fact that many religions are harmful to society. But they are wrong to lump the existence of God and true Christianity in with the rest of the lot. New Testament Christianity is unique, logically valid, historically documented, and philosophically flawless. It does not crumble with other religions that are filled with "vain babblings and contradictions of what is falsely called knowledge."[4] On the contrary, New Testament Christianity, as personified in the life of Jesus Christ, shines as **the truth** that makes men free.[5]

CHAPTER NOTES

1. *God Is Not Great*, p. 6.
2. Romans 1:20
3. *God Is Not Great*, p. 126.
4. 1 Timothy 6:20
5. John 8:32

Always Be Ready

"Christians Can't Even Agree With Each Other"

In my debate with Dan Barker, he stated that one good reason God "probably doesn't exist" is because, "There is no agreement among believers as to the nature or the moral principles of this God that they are arguing for. They all differ with each other." According to Dan, since those who call themselves Christians come down on both sides of moral issues such as abortion, divorce, and the death penalty, then the God Who wrote the Bible "in all probability" does not exist, and the Bible must not be a sufficient guide for human morality.

Is Dan right that disagreement among believers proves God does not exist? No, he is not. In fact, this idea is incorrect for a number of reasons. First, we could simply say that this "no agreement" argument refutes itself, since atheists disagree as well. In his book *Godless,* Barker stated: "**Most** atheists think that values, though not objective things in themselves, can be objectively justified by reference to the real world.... Although **most** atheists accept the importance of morality, this is not conceding that morality exists in the universe."[1] Notice that Barker says that "most" atheists accept morality. But he admits some do not see the situation as he does.

In his discussion of human free will, Barker wrote: "By the way, this contributes to my compatibilist position

on human free will. (**Not that all atheists agree with me**.) I am a determinist, which means that I don't think complete libertarian free will exists.... **I admit that my definition of free will is subject to debate.**"[2] If Barker's statement about disagreement of professed believers is true, we could use it on atheism and say that since there is no agreement among atheists on moral issues, then atheism "in all probability" is false.

The second problem with this atheistic argument is simply that it is false. If two or more people disagreed on whether the holocaust happened, but they all professed to be honest historians, would their disagreement prove that the holocaust never happened? If two people, who both claim to be honest geographers, disagree on the fact that the continent of North America exists, would that negate its reality? The answer is "No" in every case. Agreement among people cannot be used as evidence of the truth or falsity of any proposition.

Another well-known atheist named Sam Harris has written about this. He disagrees with many atheists about ethical questions. In spite of his atheism, he contends that objective right and wrong do exist (an impossible proposition for a true atheist to maintain, by the way). He wrote:

> The fact that people of different times and cultures disagree about ethical questions should not trouble us. **It suggests nothing at all about the status of moral truth**. Imagine what it would be like to consult the finest thinkers of antiquity on questions of basic science: "What," we might ask, "is fire? And how do living systems reproduce themselves? And what are the various lights we see in the night sky?" We would surely encounter a bewildering lack of consensus on these matters. Even though there was no shortage of brilliant minds in the ancient world, they simply lacked the physical and conceptual tools to answer

questions of this sort. **Their lack of consensus signified their ignorance of certain physical truths, not that no such truths exist.**[3]

Harris' statement hammers home the truth that agreement has no bearing on truth. Harris further remarked: "It is quite conceivable that everyone might agree and yet be wrong about the way the world is. It is also conceivable that a **single person might be right in the face of unanimous opposition.**"[4]

The lack of agreement on moral issues by those who profess Christianity does nothing to discount the existence of God. But why does such disagreement exists? It is ironic that Dan Barker has answered this question for us. In his speech, "How to be Moral Without Religion," given at the University of Minnesota on October 19, 2006, Barker stated: "A tendency that we all have, we look through our documents to try to find what supports **our already prejudice views** about what **we think morality should be like.**" In one succinct sentence, Barker explained why there is a lack of consensus among professed believers on moral issues. It is not because God does not exist. It is not because the Bible is hopelessly confusing and cannot be understood. It is not because there is no objective moral truth. It is simply because humans bring **their already prejudice views** to the text of the Bible and try to force it to say what they "think" it should say.

CHAPTER NOTES

1. *Godless*, pp. 213-214.
2. *Godless*, p. 128.
3. *The End of Faith*, p. 172.
4. *The End of Faith*, pp. 181-182.

Always Be Ready

"Creationists Don't Publish Their Research in Scientific Journals"

Those of us who believe that God created the Universe are often ridiculed by evolutionary scientists. This ridicule comes in many different forms, but one of the most often used tactics is to claim that creation science is simply not good science. As "evidence" that creation or intelligent design is not "good science," atheistic evolutionists brag about the fact that peer-reviewed scientific journals do not publish papers that support intelligent design. A couple of sample statements to this effect follow:

- "ID [Intelligent Design—KB] advocates complain that their views are rejected out of hand by the scientific establishment, yet they do not play by the normal rules of presenting their views first through scientific conferences and then to peer-reviewed journals and then in textbooks."[1]
- "Most telling, perhaps, is intelligent design's near total failure to make any headway in the peer-reviewed publications that are the gateway to scientific success."[2]

The reasoning here is that if creation or intelligent design were scientific, then it would be included in peer-reviewed journals. Since it does not appear in peer reviewed journals, then it must be unscientific. The problem with this reasoning is the circular process by which papers are accepted for inclusion in such journals. Scientists in authoritative positions have established their own definition for science.

"To be scientific in our era is to search for **solely natural explanations.**"[3] The National Academy of Sciences says: "The statements of science must invoke only **natural** things and processes."[4] Thus, if a paper even hints at something other than a "natural" explanation, it is rejected as "unscientific" regardless of the facts or research involved in the paper. Creationists' papers are not allowed in peer-reviewed journals, not because they are poorly written or documented, but because they do not offer "solely natural explanations."

An example of this prejudicial dismissal of intelligent design material occurred in 2004. In that year, Richard Sternberg allowed a paper that presented evidence in favor of intelligent design to be published in a peer-reviewed journal. Concerning what happened as a result, Sternberg wrote:

> In 2004, in my capacity as editor of *The Proceedings of the Biological Society of Washington*, I authorized "The Origin of Biological Information and the Higher Taxonomic Categories" by Dr. Stephen Meyer to be published in the journal after passing peer-review. Because Dr. Meyer's article presented scientific evidence for intelligent design in biology, I faced retaliation, defamation, harassment, and a hostile work environment at the Smithsonian's National Museum of Natural History that was designed to force me out as a Research Associate there.[5]

Reacting to the fact that an intelligent design paper was published in the journal, The Council of the Biological Society of Washington that sponsors the journal wrote an official statement concerning the ordeal. It wrote:

> The paper by Stephen C. Meyer...was published at the discretion of the former editor Richard v. [sic] Sternberg. Contrary to typical editorial practices, the paper was published without review by any associate editor; associate editors would have deemed the paper inappropriate for

> the pages of the *Proceedings* because the subject matter represents such a significant departure from the nearly purely systematic content for which this journal has been known throughout its 122-year history.... The Council endorses a resolution on ID published by the American Association for the Advancement of Science...which observes that there is no credible scientific evidence supporting ID as a testable hypothesis to explain the origin of organic diversity. Accordingly, the Meyer paper does not meet the scientific standards of the *Proceedings*.[6]

The way the council presents the matter, it seems that Sternberg did not go through the proper peer-review process. But that is not the case. The article was peer-reviewed and revised in accordance with the reviewers' suggestions. The article did not cause a stir because it did not pass the review process. It caused a stir because it did not meet the "scientific standard"—in other words, because it advocated the possibility of an Intelligent Designer.

The Council alluded to a resolution on Intelligent Design issued by the American Association for the Advancement of Science. That resolution was adopted in October of 2002. In that resolution, the AAAS stated: "*Therefore Be It Further Resolved*, that AAAS calls upon its members to assist those engaged in overseeing science education policy to understand the nature of science, the content of contemporary evolutionary theory and the inappropriateness of 'intelligent design theory' as subject matter."[7] This simply means that if any book, article, or paper has anything about intelligent design in it, do not publish, promote, or condone it in anyway.

Thus, it is clear that the oft-repeated accusation against creation science's lack of peer-reviewed papers is seen for what it is, an intentional exclusion based, not on the merits

of the paper, but on the agreed-upon (but false) definition that true science involves only "natural explanations."

The scientific establishment's stance is similar to that of a child who forms an exclusive club. One of the rules for membership of the club is that all members must be "extremely smart." The child then includes in the by-laws the statement that all smart people should think that he (the founding member) is always right. Thus, he concludes that those who do not think he is always right are not smart. Then, he proceeds to malign those not in the club based on the idea that they are not smart. And as proof that they are not smart, he states that it is obvious they are not smart because they are not members of his club. In truth, his real motivation for slandering those outside his club is simply the fact that they disagree with him. This is the same motivation that propels the evolutionary establishment to reject all creation science articles. You will not see articles advocating intelligent design in the majority of peer-reviewed journals, not because the findings are unscientific, not because they fail to provide evidence and proof of their conclusions, but because they are not atheistic and evolutionary.

CHAPTER NOTES

1. Eugenie Scott made this statement in a book titled *Not in Our Classrooms*, p. 22.
2. A statement by Jay Wexler in *Not in Our Classrooms*, p. 94.
3. Martinez Hewlett and Ted Peters, *Not in Our Classrooms*, p. 75.
4. *Teaching About Evolution*, p. 42.
5. He made this statement in an article titled: "Smithsonian Controversy." You can access it on-line at: http://www.richardsternberg.com/smithsonian.php.
6. "Statement from the Council of the Biological Society of Washington" at http://www.biodiversitylibrary.org/page/35515694/#page/262/mode/1up.
7. "AAAS Board Resolution on Intelligent Design Theory" at http://www.aaas.org/news/releases/2002/1106id2.shtml.

Chapter 16

"Everything in the Universe is Made of Matter or Energy"

The *American Heritage Dictionary* defines **materialism** as, "The theory that physical matter is the only reality and that everything, including thought, feeling, mind, and will, can be explained in terms of matter and physical phenomena." Evolutionist Paul Davies wrote: "The materialist believes that mental states and operation are nothing but physical states and operations."[1] In short, there is an idea prevalent among atheists that matter is the only "real" thing that exists. According to this view, if it is not material or physical, then it is not a part of the Universe, and is either non-existent or unimportant.

The major problem with this idea is the fact that we can easily show that some things do exist which are not material. Among the most obvious of those is information. In a book titled *In Six Days*, Nancy M. Darrall gives an excellent summary of the problem that information poses to the theory of materialism.[2] For instance, suppose that etched in the sand of the beach are the words, "Sam is six feet tall." A passerby reads that message, calls his wife, and says over the phone, "Sam is six feet tall." His wife sits down and writes a letter to her sister, in which she pens the words, "Sam is six feet tall." Her sister, who happens to be deaf, reads the letter and says to her husband in sign language, "Sam is six feet tall." Her husband watches the

signs, translates the message into Spanish, and records it on a CD. A man who writes sky messages hears the CD, gets into his plane and scrolls in the sky, "Sam is six feet tall," in English. The man standing on the beach who originally phoned his wife sees the message in the sky, looks down at the sentence on the beach, and accurately notes that the two messages contain the same information.

Now, let's look at our scenario. First, the sand where the message started did not inherently contain the information. In other words, the message is not part of the physical make-up of the grains of sand. The message could be read without ever touching the sand. Second, the message was sent through telephone lines that did not inherently contain the information, since the message was in the husband's mind before he picked up the phone, and none of his brains cells was sent through the phone line. Third, the information cannot be linked to the physical properties of the pen, ink, or paper, since the message was in the mind of the wife before she started writing. Fourth, when the information was passed using sign language, no physical contact was made, yet the information was accurately transferred. Finally, the sky-written message contained the same information as the message in the sand, and any average adult could come to that conclusion.

What does all this prove? It proves that information is not material or physical. It is something that can be transferred through matter like pen, ink, voice, sand, air, etc. But its substance is something completely different from the medium used to convey the message. Millions of processes everyday deal strictly with information—from DNA to desktop computers. This information can be transferred, translated, decoded, and encoded into a

host of different physical media without ever altering the actual information.

So what does that mean? If information is not material, and information does exist, then some things that are not material **do exist**, and materialism is false. One of those immaterial beings is God. The Bible says that God is spirit.[3] He is the great Knower, the master Giver of information, Who sustains all things by "the word of His power."[4]

CHAPTER NOTES

1. *God and the New Physics*, p. 82.
2. *In Six Days: Why Fifty Scientists Choose to Believe in Creation*, pp. 182-199.
3. John 4:24
4. Hebrews 1:3

Chapter 17

All the Smart People

Many people choose to believe in evolution because they have been told that "all" the smart people believe in atheistic evolution. They have been led to believe that all the educated, elite scientists and specialists in their fields accept the idea. Atheist Richard Dawkins once stated: "It is absolutely safe to say that if you meet somebody who claims not to believe in evolution, that person is ignorant, stupid, or insane (or wicked, but I'd rather not consider that)."[1] Dawkins is saying that smart, sane, knowledgeable, and noble people believe in evolution. In fact, one of the most powerful arguments used by evolutionists and atheists to convince people to believe their teaching is the false idea that "all smart people believe in evolution," or that "all scientists" believe in evolution. Statements made by Darwinian evolutionists often suggest that evolution is believed by the intelligent people. Notice this brief list of such statements:

- "Evolution is a **fact**, like digestion."[2]
- "Evolution of the animal and plant world is considered by **all those entitled to a judgment** to be a fact for which no further proof is needed."[3]
- "The first point to make about Darwin's theory is that it is no longer a theory, but a fact. **No serious scientist** would deny the **fact** that evolution has occurred."[4]
- "By now, scientists say, evolution is no longer 'just a theory.' It's an everyday phenomenon, **a fundamental**

fact of biology as real as hunger and as unavoidable as death."[5]

- "No **educated person** any longer questions the validity of the so-called theory of evolution, which we now know to be a simple fact."[6]

A list of this type could go on for hundreds of pages, documenting all the various ways the public is pressured to believe that modern science, at least that done by competent, educated, serious scientists entitled to a judgment, accepts Darwinian evolution.

The truth of the matter is, however, not all intelligent, educated, serious scientists accept Darwinian evolution. In fact, thousands of extremely well-educated men and women all over the world are willing to stand up and be counted as those who do not believe in Darwinian evolution. Jerry Bergman has amassed a list of more than 3,000 individuals, many of whom have Ph.D.s in science.[7] Bergman stated: "I estimate that, given the time and resources, I could easily complete a list of 10,000 names." He also noted: "On my list I have well over 3,000 names including Nobel Prize winners but, unfortunately, a large number of persons that could be added to the public list, including many college professors, did not want their name listed because of real concerns over possible retaliation or harm to their careers."

Hundreds of names of scientists could be added to this list, such as Dr. John Baumgardner, whose theory on plate tectonics was reported in *Nature*. Dr. Raymond Jones was described as one of the top scientists in Australia. Dr. Brian Stone has received numerous awards in his engineering field. Raymond Damadian helped to invent MRI [magnetic resonance imaging].[8] Dr. A.E. Wilder-Smith held three earned doctorates from three European universities. Dr. Melvin A. Cook won the 1968 E.G. Murphee Award in

Industrial and Engineering Chemistry from the American Chemical Society. Dimitri Kouznetsov, M.D, Ph.D., D.Sc., won the Komsomol Lenin Prize in 1983, and distinguished himself as one of the two most promising scientists in Russia at the time.[9]

While creationists may be in the minority when it comes to the sciences, they certainly leave a most impressive mark. Of course, this discussion is in no way intended to sway anyone to believe in creation or the existence of God based on the views held by the "smart people" mentioned above. It **is** intended to report the truth that many intelligent thinkers have found "holes" in the ideas of evolution and atheism. It does not take a rocket scientist to see the flaws in evolution, but many rocket scientists can see them—as well as biologists, geologists, and chemists. Truly smart people do away with any faulty appeals to authority, and simply look at the evidence.

CHAPTER NOTES

1. This statement is on record in *The New York Times*, April 9, 1989, section 7, p. 34.
2. W.W. Howells in *Mankind So Far*, p. 5.
3. Richard Goldschmidt in "Evolution, As Viewed By One Geneticist," in *American Scientist*, 1952, volume 40, p. 84.
4. Julian Huxley in *Issues in Evolution*, p. 41.
5. Thomas Hayden made this statement in an article titled, "A Theory Evolves," that was published in the July 29, 2002 issue of *U.S. News and World Report*, on pp. 42-50.
6. Evolutionist Ernst Mayer made this statement. It is recorded by Jerry Bergman in an article titled, "Darwin Skeptics." You can find it on-line at: http://www.rae.org/darwinskeptics.htm.
7. You can find that list here: http://www.rae.org/darwinskeptics.html.
8. For this list, see Jonathan Sarfati's book *Refuting Evolution*, pp. 26-27.
9. Duane Gish documents this in his book *Evolution: The Fossils Still Say No!*, on pp. 13-14.

Chapter 18

Never Enough Evidence

"How can a person refuse to believe in God in the face of so much evidence that proves His existence?" In my travels and experiences teaching Christian evidences, this question often arises. Many who look at the evidence for the existence of God, the inspiration of the Bible, and the deity of Christ, simply cannot understand how a person could deny these truths. Why doesn't the force of such evidence compel all those who hear it to become believers in God and the Bible?

The simple answer to such a question is that some people have decided not to believe the truth about God and the Bible, regardless of how much evidence is presented. The story of the resurrection of Lazarus provides a perfect biblical illustration of this attitude. In John 11, the Bible records the facts regarding one of Jesus' more spectacular miracles. His friend Lazarus became sick and died. The dead man's body was buried in a tomb and remained there for four days. Mary and Martha, Lazarus' sisters, were deeply grieved over the loss of their brother. When Jesus arrived in the city, He asked to be taken to the tomb. He then instructed those at the tomb to remove the stone covering the entrance. Martha attempted to discourage Jesus from this course of action by informing Him that her dead brother's body had been in the tomb four days and was decayed to the point that his body would stink. Yet, in

an awesome show of God's power over death, Jesus called Lazarus forth from the grave, bringing him back to life.

By bringing Lazarus back to life, Jesus provided evidence that proved He is God's Son. Such evidence should have been enough for any honest observer to conclude that Jesus was from God. In fact, the Jewish leaders admitted that Jesus worked many signs.[1] Because of these signs, they were afraid that all the people would believe in Jesus if He continued His ministry. What, then, was their reaction to the signs that Jesus performed? In John 12:10-11, the Bible says: "But the chief priests took counsel that they might also put Lazarus to death, because on account of him many of the Jews went away and believed in Jesus."

These villainous leaders were not motivated to honestly assess the evidence and believe in Jesus. In fact, in order to keep others from doing so, they considered killing an innocent man—Lazarus—simply because his life provided evidence of Jesus' deity. They knew Jesus raised him from the dead, but refused to allow this evidence to change their beliefs and actions. Such is still the case today. Those who refuse to accept the evidence that proves God's existence, the Bible's inspiration, and the deity of Christ do so based on a predetermined bias and not an honest look at the facts.

When I debated Dan Barker, we had a period of time when audience members could ask each of us questions. One member of the audience asked Dan what kind of evidence it would take to prove atheism wrong. Dan responded by saying:

> If Kyle were to pray and ask God to predict something, and Kyle were to turn to me and say, God told me, Dan, tomorrow at 12:14 P.M., a meteorite from the southwest at 85 degrees would strike your house—not my house—go through the Navajo rug on the second floor, go down into the basement and end up 17 inches below the basement

> floor composed of 72% iron, 1% iridium, 3% nickel and so on. And then if that happens exactly as you told me that God told you or predicted, I would say, "Oops, my atheism is falsified," right?
>
> So I could—if Jesus were to materialize on this stage—he did it before, according to your belief system; he materialized through solid door and he floated into the sky. If he were to materialize here and speak to us and tell us the exact geographical coordinates where the ark of the covenant is buried in Jerusalem, in the Holy Land, and if we were to go over there to that point and dig it up and find it, I would say, "Oops, atheism is wrong." I could come up with a lot of stuff like that.

The truth is, God has predicted the future in detail, and yet Barker has not believed in Him.[2] Barker is right, Jesus did materialize in a room where the apostles were hiding, but Barker does not accept that as evidence against atheism. God has talked directly to people in the past and told them things that were absolutely true, but Barker refuses to acknowledge those encounters as evidence that falsifies atheism.

In the debate, I responded to Barker by saying:

> Let me tell you this. Here has historically been what has always happened. The person who has chosen not to believe always says, "If I had just a little more evidence, then I would believe." In John chapter 11, after Jesus raised Lazarus from the dead, the Jewish community looked at that miracle and said: "Now we believe in Jesus?" No. They said: "Now people are believing in Jesus, so we have got to kill Lazarus."
>
> When Jesus Christ was on the cross, do you remember what they said? They said, "If you will come down from there, we will believe." They had not believed when He made blind Bartimaeus see. They had not believed when the things that had been predicted about His life came

> true—born in Bethlehem of a virgin, going into the city of Jerusalem on—all of those things. Just a little bit more.... Always more information.

No one believes in atheism **because of the evidence**, but in spite of the evidence. That is why the inspired apostle Paul noted that people who deny the existence of God will be "without excuse" on the Day of Judgment.[3]

Chapter Notes

1. John 11:47
2. See chapters 8, 9, and 10 of my book *Behold! The Word of God*. You can download it free from the A.P. Web site at: http://www.apologeticspress.org/pdfs/e-books_pdf/Behold%20the%20Word%20of%20God.pdf.
3. Romans 1:20

Conclusion

Madalyn Murray O'Hair was the founder of the American Atheist organization. She lived a life in complete rebellion against her God. Her rabid atheism prodded her to attack the idea of God whenever she could. But her atheism could not bring her joy, and it could not show her love. When her personal belongings were auctioned, it was discovered that several times in her writings she penned the heartbreaking cry: "Somebody, somewhere, love me!" The greatest tragedy of atheism is that it strips the world of everything meaningful and loving. Atheist Dan Barker admitted that, according to atheism, "In the end of the cosmos it's not going to matter. You and I are like ants or rats or like pieces of broccoli, really, in the big picture... there is no value to our species...we are no different than a piece of broccoli in the cosmic sense."[1]

According to atheism, humans are nothing more than matter in motion. Our actions will not determine where we spend eternity. And any "feeling" that one person may have for another person can only be "skin deep." It can only be a product of the physical brain. As much as atheists try to discuss love, they cannot explain how it can exist in a world without God.

Sadly, just like O'Hair, there is a world full of people who want someone to love them, but they refuse to recognize that there is Someone out there Who does. Their Creator, God, loves them so much that He came to die on the cross

for them. Jesus Christ, God in the flesh, gave His life to prove His love for humanity. And He gave His life so that those humans who choose to obey Him can live eternally in heaven. "For God so loved the world that He gave His only begotten Son, that whoever believes in Him should not perish but have everlasting life."[2]

But God's love has a limit. He will not force anyone to believe in Him. He loves each person enough to let us all freely choose whether or not to believe in and obey Him. And our choice will determine our eternal destiny. Moses once wrote to the Israelites: "I call heaven and earth as witnesses today against you, that I have set before you life and death, blessing and cursing; therefore choose life."[3] The failure to choose the right beliefs and actions in this life has real consequences.

We are not ultimately like broccoli or rats. Our decisions really matter, for now and for eternity. Those who refuse to acknowledge God can have no hope for an afterlife or joy in death. Agnostic Bart Ehrman, who once claimed to be a Christian, wrote: "The fear of death gripped me for years, **and there are still moments when I wake up at night in a cold sweat.**"[4] The Bible explains that Christ came to defeat death, and "release those who through fear of death were all their lifetime subject to bondage."[5] The only solution to the fear of death and the emptiness felt without God is to seek Him and His will. Madalyn Murray O'Hair's cry, "Somebody, somewhere, love me!" echoes across the world from millions of voices who are trying to find love apart from God. The irony of it all is that they have shut their ears to the voice of God, Who through His Son, calls from the cross, "I love you."

CHAPTER NOTES

1. This is a quote from his debate with Paul Monata on the radio program, "The Infidel Guy."
2. John 3:16. For a more complete discussion about obeying God's plan of salvation, see the Apologetics Press booklet *Receiving The Gift of Salvation* at this link: http://www.apologeticspress.org/pdfs/e-books_pdf/Receiving%20the%20Gift%20of%20Salvation.pdf
3. Deuteronomy 30:19
4. *God's Problem*, p. 127
5. Hebrews 2:15